GENESIS

Origin of God's Chosen Nation

Mitch Robison

Charleston, AR

2020

Genesis: Origin of God's Chosen Nation
is copyright 2020 © Mitch Robison.
All rights reserved.

No portion of this book may be reproduced in any way without the prior written permission of the author.

The material in this book was designed to be used in teaching the book of Genesis to others. May God get the glory for any benefit that you can derive from this book.

These notes are the result of an in-depth study of God's word. That study was assisted by use of several commentaries, books, and other notes from years of education and training. What you have here is the most pertinent information (in my opinion) that will allow you to feel confident in your knowledge of this portion of Scripture.

All the glory goes to God!

Published in the United States of America by:
Cobb Publishing
www.CobbPublishing.com
CobbPublishing@gmail.com
479.747.8372
ISBN: 978-1-947622-44-9

Dedication

*This book, and the work that I do, is dedicated to
the three souls whom I cherish more than any.*

*To Katy, my wife,
I am thankful for your support throughout the years.
You encourage me to pursue my mission.
You serve as a great wife and mother of our children.
You are a great encouragement to the church and add great value to it.
I love you!*

*To my children, Sadie and Eli,
who are beautiful in so many ways, this is for you as well.
My hope as a father has been to leave something in this world
that would help you through life.
The material in this book will help to strengthen your faith
and ability to give a defense for the truth.
It is my prayer that you will live faithfully for the Lord,
that you will honor your mother and me,
that you will forever love each other,
and that you will serve those around you
in an effort to shine your light for Christ.
I am so proud of you both
and I love you more than words can express.*

Contents

Intro to the Course	1
Reasons for Studying the Old Testament	1
Purpose of Old Testament	2
Divisions and Books of the Old Testament	2
Periods of Old Testament History	3
God's Redemption Found In the Scripture	5
Christ in the Book of Genesis	5
Hypotheses of Creation	6
Methods of Estimating the Earth's Antiquity	6
A Little More on Origins	7
Background Info on Genesis	10
Genesis – The Book Of Beginnings	11
Intro to the Course	1
Reasons for Studying the Old Testament	1
Purpose of Old Testament	2
Divisions and Books of the Old Testament	2
Periods of Old Testament History	3
God's Redemption Found In the Scripture	5
Christ in the Book of Genesis	5
Hypotheses of Creation	6
Methods of Estimating the Earth's Antiquity	6
A Little More on Origins	7
Background Info on Genesis	10
Genesis – The Book Of Beginnings	11
The History of Creation	12
The History of Creation – Continued	16
Life In God's Garden	17
The Days of Creation	19
The Temptation and Fall of Man	21
Cain Murders Abel	25
The Family of Cain	26
A New Son	27
The Family of Adam	28
The Wickedness and Judgment of Man	30
Noah Pleases God	32
The Ark Prepared	32
The Great Flood	34
Noah's Deliverance	36
God's Covenant with Creation	36
God's Promise to Noah	38
Noah and His Sons	39
Nations Descended From Noah	41
The Tower of Babel	42
Shem's Descendants	43
Terah's Descendants	43
Promises to Abram	44
Abram in Egypt	45
Abram Inherits Canaan	47
Lot's Captivity and Rescue	49

Abram and Melchizedek	49
God's Covenant with Abram	51
Hagar and Ishmael	53
The Sign of the Covenant	56
The Son of Promise	58
Abraham Intercedes For Sodom	59
Sodom's Depravity	61
Sodom and Gomorrah Destroyed	62
The Descendants of Lot	63
Abraham and Abimelech	64
Isaac Is Born	65
Hagar and Ishmael Depart	65
A Covenant with Abimelech	66
Abraham's Faith Confirmed	68
The Family of Nahor	70
Sarah's Death and Burial	71
A Bride For Isaac	72
Abraham and Keturah	75
Abraham's Death and Burial	75
The Families of Ishmael and Isaac	76
Esau Sells His Birthright	77
Isaac and Abimelech	78
Isaac Blesses Jacob	81
Esau's Lost Hope	82
Jacob Escapes from Esau	82
Jacob escapes from Esau Cont'd	84
Esau Marries Mahalath	84
Jacob's Vow at Bethel	84
Jacob Meets Rachel	86
Jacob Marries Leah and Rachel	86
The Children of Jacob	87
The Children of Jacob Cont'd	88
Jacob's Agreement With Laban	89
Jacob Flees From Laban	91
Laban Pursues Jacob	92
Laban's Covenant with Jacob	93
Esau comes to meet Jacob	95
Wrestling With God	96
Jacob and Esau Meet	97
Jacob Comes to Canaan	98
The Dinah Incident	99
Jacob's Return to Bethel	102
Death of Rachel	103
Jacob's Twelve Sons	103
Death of Isaac	104
The Family of Esau	105
The Chiefs of Edom	105
The Sons of Seir	105
The King of Edom	106
The Chiefs of Esau	106
Joseph Dreams of Greatness	107
Joseph Sold By His Brothers	108
Judah and Tamar	110

Joseph a Slave in Egypt	113
The Prisoners' Dreams	116
Pharaoh's Dreams	118
Joseph's Rise to Power	118
Joseph's Brothers Go To Egypt	120
The Brothers Return to Canaan	121
Joseph's Brothers Return With Benjamin	123
Joseph's Cup	126
Judah Intercedes for Benjamin	127
Joseph Revealed to His Brothers	128
Jacob's Journey to Egypt	130
Jacob Settles In Goshen	131
Jacob Settles In Goshen Cont'd	133
Joseph Deals with the Famine	134
Joseph's Vow to Jacob	134
Jacob Blesses Joseph's Sons	135
Jacob's Last Words to His Sons	137
Jacob's Death	139
Burial of Jacob	140
Joseph Reassures His Brothers	141
Death of Joseph	142

Old Testament & Genesis – Introduction

Intro to the Course

We are going to begin by talking about some things that may not necessarily be related to Genesis, but are important to understand while studying Scriptures, in particular, the Old Testament.

*When we do get to the text, it will be important that you read at home, so that you will be prepared for the class.

** I use the NKJV.

Reasons for Studying the Old Testament

1. It tells many things about God and His nature not found in any other place. **e.g.** God's attitude toward worshiping Him in any way other than that which He has commanded.
   a. God wants to be worshipped.
   b. We must not change His pattern for worship.
   c. There are many examples in the OT and NT of people not worshipping correctly.

2. It shows many things about man and his nature not found in any other place. **e.g.** How he came into being (our creation) and how he fell into sin (how we were forced out of the garden).

3. It tells of the origin, nature, and consequences of sin.
   - No other writing can make that claim unless it quotes the Bible as its source.

4. It reveals the greatest religious teachings found anywhere outside the New Testament. **e.g.** Other religions are founded on it – Mohammedanism, Modern Judaism.
   - These are false religions.

5. It presents the highest moral and ethical standards found anywhere outside the New Testament. **e.g.** Other religious books of the time (and nearly all other times) have glorified & exalted immorality either in man or their gods.

6. It aids in developing a spiritual and devotional life.
   - These are examples.
     - *But with most of them God was not well pleased, for their bodies were scattered in the wilderness. Now these things became our examples, to the intent that we should not lust after evil things as they also lusted (1 Corinthians 10:5-6).*
   - These are given for our learning.

- *For whatever things were written before were written for our learning, that we through the patience and comfort of the Scriptures might have hope (Romans 15:4).*

7. It helps one to solve many practical problems in family life, economics, national or civic relationships, education of children, etc. **e.g.** Isaac and Jacob using deceit which had first shown up in their father Abraham.

- Abraham, when questioned about Sarah, said that she was not his wife, but his sister.

8. It has historical information not known from any other source. **e.g.** Origin and history of the Jewish nation. Israel was small compared to other nations, so secular history overlooked them.

9. It gives the <u>only true</u> account of God's people and His actions in this world. **e.g.** Babylon and the flood accounts.

- We have other accounts, but they are not dependable.

10. It contains some of the finest examples of literary excellence known in the world.

- It is finely written, especially for the times.
- It is inspired by God, but men were used to write it.

11. It gives necessary background for the understanding of the New Testament. **e.g.** The argument made by the writer of the book of Hebrews based on Melchizedek would almost be valueless without that knowledge.

Purpose of Old Testament

First Purpose:

- *Therefore by the deeds of the law no flesh will be justified in His sight, for by the law is the knowledge of sin (Romans 3:20).*
- *What purpose then does the law serve? It was added because of transgressions, till the Seed should come to whom the promise was made; and it was appointed through angels by the hand of a mediator (Galatians 3:19).*

Second Purpose:

- *Therefore the law was our tutor to bring us to Christ, that we might be justified by faith (Galatians 3:24).*
- The OT brings us to an understanding that will ultimately bring us to Christ.

Divisions and Books of the Old Testament

Pentateuch (Books of Moses) – 5 total
(1) Genesis (2) Exodus (3) Leviticus (4) Numbers (5) Deuteronomy

History – 12 total
(6) Joshua (7) Judges (8) Ruth (9) 1 Samuel (10) 2 Samuel (11) 1 Kings
(12) 2 Kings (13) 1 Chronicles (14) 2 Chronicles (15) Ezra (16) Nehemiah   (17) Esther

Wisdom Literature (Poetry) – 5 total
(18) Job (19) Psalms (20) Proverbs (21) Ecclesiastes
(22) Song of Solomon (Song of Songs)

Major Prophets (Because they are bigger) – 5 total
(23) Isaiah (24) Jeremiah (25) Lamentations (26) Ezekiel (27) Daniel

Minor Prophets – 12 total
(28) Hosea (29) Joel (30) Amos (31) Obadiah (32) Johan (33) Micah (34) Nahum
(35) Habakkuk (36) Zephaniah (37) Haggai (38) Zechariah (39) Malachi

Periods of Old Testament History

Sometimes when we read about these events we tend to shorten them up some in our minds. But there are a lot of years that go by in some of the stories of the Old Testament.

1. **Ante-Diluvian Period** – 4004-2348 B.C. – 1656 Years (Estimate. Not sure of exact date of creation)

    a. From creation to the flood
    b. Genesis Ch. 1-7
    c. This word means "before the flood." Principle characters: Adam and Eve and their sons, Cain, Abel and Seth. It follows the line of Seth to Noah.

2. **Post-Diluvian Period** – 2348-1921 B.C. – 427 Years

    a. From the flood to the call of Abram
    b. Genesis Ch. 8-11
    c. This word means "after the flood." Noah, his wife and their three sons: Shem, Ham, and Japheth with their three wives repopulate the earth. This period is concerned with the descendants of Shem.

3. **Patriarchal Period** – 1921-1706 B.C. – 215 Years

    a. From the call of Abram to the migration to Egypt.
    b. Genesis Ch. 12-45, time of the book of Job.
    c. This period is centered around the great patriarchs of Israel: Abraham, Isaac, Jacob, and the early life of Jacob's twelve sons.

4. **Egyptian Bondage** – 1706-1491 B.C. – 215 Years

    a. From the migration to Egypt to the Exodus.
    b. Genesis Ch. 45 – Exodus Ch. 11
    c. Joseph, now a prominent person in Egypt, makes arrangements for his father and eleven brothers to live in Egypt where they will grow to be a great nation.

5. **Time in the Wilderness (Wilderness Wanderings)** – 1491-1451 B.C. – 40 Years

    a. From the Exodus to the crossing of the Jordan River.
    b. Genesis 45 through Leviticus, Numbers, and Deuteronomy.

    c. Moses (with the help of God) delivered Israel from Egyptian oppression, led them across the Red Sea, and gave them the Law at Sinai. Because of unbelief, Israel had forty years of waiting before they were allowed to enter the Promised Land.

6. **Conquest of Canaan** – 1451-1400 B.C. – 51 Years

   a. From the crossing of the Jordan River to the death of Joshua.
   b. Book of Joshua
   c. After Moses' death on Mt. Nebo, Joshua led Israel across the Jordan into Canaan and conquered the seven nations in Canaan, thereby possessing the land promised to Abraham's seed.

7. **Period of Judges** – 1400-1095 B.C. – 305 Years

   a. From the death of Joshua to the anointing of Saul.
   b. Judges – 1 Samuel, Ruth written at this time.
   c. God allowed Israel to be oppressed when she was wicked, and He delivered her by a judge when she repented. The judges were: Othniel, Ehud, Shamgar, Deborah, Gideon, Abimelech, Tola, Jair, Jephthah, Ibzan, Elon, Abdon, Samson, Eli, and Samuel (the judge and prophet).
   d. These were not judges as we think of them today. They were leaders – primarily military leaders. They were to bring the people out of bondage and back to the Lord.
   e. The pattern in Judges is an example of the pattern of many today. Salvation, sin, servitude (consequence of their sin), supplication.

8. **The United Kingdom** – 1095-975 B.C. – 120 Years

   a. From the anointing of Saul to the death of Solomon.
   b. 1 Samuel 9 – 1 Kings 11, also 1 Chronicles 10 – 2 Chronicles 9. Psalms, Proverbs, Song of Solomon, and Ecclesiastes written.
   c. This period was ruled over by three kings: Saul, David, and Solomon. Israel's desire to have a king like the nations around her caused her much grief.

9. **The Divided Kingdom** – 975-722 B.C. – 253 Years

   a. From the death of Solomon to the fall of Israel.
   b. 1 Kings 12 – 2 Kings 17, also 2 Chronicles 10-32. Obadiah, Joel, Jonah, Amos, Hosea, Isaiah, and Nahum written.
   c. When Solomon died, the kingdom was divided between ten tribes (Northern—Israel) and two tribes (Southern—Judah). Elijah, Ahab, Jezebel, Elisha, and Jehu lived during this time.

10. **Kingdom of Judah Alone** – 722-586 B.C. – 136 Years

    a. From the fall of Israel to the Fall of Jerusalem.
    b. 2 Kings 18-25, also 2 Chronicles 33-36. Habakkuk, Zephaniah, Nahum, Jeremiah, and Lamentations written.
    c. Because of ungodliness, Israel (Northern Kingdom) carried away by the Assyrians. Isaiah, Hezekiah, and Joshua lived.

11. **Babylonian Captivity** – 586 (When Temple destroyed) – 536 B.C. – 50 Years (Actual captivity was 70 years)

1. From the fall of Jerusalem to the rebuilding of the Temple.
2. 2 Kings 25:8-21. Ezekiel and Daniel were written.
3. 112 years after the fall of Israel, Babylon captured Assyria. Because of Judah's increased wickedness she also went into Babylon captivity.

12. **Restoration of the Jews** – 536-400 B.C. – 136 Years
    a. From the rebuilding of the Temple to the close of the OT.
    b. Ezra, Nehemiah, Esther, Haggai, Zechariah, and Malachi written.
    c. The decree of Cyrus permitted the return of the Jews (Judah). The first group was led by Zerubbabel and they began to rebuild the Temple. A second group was led by Ezra. Nehemiah completed the return, which took 92 years in all.

God's Redemption Found In the Scripture

Planned before creation – Ephesians 1:3-4; 2 Timothy 1:9 – God knew that man would fall. God had a plan of redemption in place.

Planned at creation – Genesis 1-4

Prepared for – The promise to Eve in 3:15; The promise to Abram in 12:1-3; The promise of Christ Himself in Malachi 4.

Effected – The Gospels

Shared – Acts

Explained – The Epistles

Realized – Revelation

God knew we would fall short. But He loved us so much that He had a plan in mind for our redemption.

Christ in the Book of Genesis

Prophecies Made:
- *World champion to come* – 3:15 – The first gospel message.
- *A descendant of Abraham* – 28:14 – But from where specifically?
- *From the tribe of Judah* – 49:10

Prophecies Fulfilled In Christ:
- *Satan bruised* – Romans 16:20; 1 Corinthians 15:24-28; Colossians 1:12-23; Revelation 12:7-12
- *Christ blesses the world* – Galatians 3:28-29; Ephesians 2
- *Christ from the tribe of Judah* – Hebrews 7:12-14

*We see in the NT that all of this has been fulfilled by our Savior.

Hypotheses of Creation

Long Chaos: Between verses one and two of Genesis chapter one there is the possibility of an infinitely long period of time, during which "the earth was waste and void."

- Evolutionists have to have <u>time</u> for their theories to work out. Not thousands or millions, but billions of years.

Creation – Ruination – Re-Creation (Restoration or Gap theory): There has been a series of worlds such as our present one. Each time God has destroyed the creation, allowed a period of chaos, and then recreated a new world.

- People suggest that there were pre-Adamic men.

Day-Age: The six "days" of the creation story really mean six long periods of time.

- Text says there is evening and morning – 1 day. How long would the "night" be if it represented a million years? What could survive during this type of cycle?
- Read John 5:45-47 and compare with Exodus 20:11.

Pictorial Day: The six days are merely a literary device to present pictorially the creation story.

- This would be deceptive. I don't believe that God is trying to deceive me. God's nature is truth.

Literal: The six days of Genesis one are six literal twenty-four hour days.

- When <u>all</u> facts and reasoning are considered we must accept the Genesis account as factual. It is the best, and only, account we have of what happened "in the beginning." All other theories are just that – theories!

True science and Scripture never contradict each other. Man's theories may, but true science does not.

Methods of Estimating the Earth's Antiquity

"Science" trying to figure it out.

1. Tree ring analysis – Say they can give estimates of time back 3000 years.
2. Varved clay analysis – "Accurate back to 15,000 years"
3. Radio-carbon dating – "Accurate to 30,000 years."
4. Percent of equilibrium method – "Radium dating accurate to 30,000 years."
5. Solar Radiation – "Accurate to 100,000 years."
6. Typical geological methods – Sedimentation, erosion factors, chemical deteriorations.
7. Uranium and radioactive methods – "Claim accuracy to 3 billion years." Now we have time for life to develop from nothing – I guess.

*Do these fit the time frame of the creation, chronologies, and genealogies given in Scripture? Approx. 6,000 years?

**We have to decide if the Bible is true or if man's theories are true.

***These are all based on the rule of uniformitarianism.

- From now back to whenever is going to be the same always.
- A certain amount of rainfall, a certain amount of radiation, etc. All this stays constant back to the beginning.
- What about floods? What about drought years? We have deserts now where cities once were.
- Things aren't always as uniform as they say it is.

See 2 Peter 3:5-6. Peter addressed this theory thousands of years before "science" came up with it.

A Little More on Origins

From the Intro to Creation Compromises:

Give a man a false, warped view of his origin, and he will likewise possess a false, warped view of his destiny. Origins and destiny are inseparably linked.

Those of us who accept the Bible as the inspired, inerrant, authoritative word of God, and who accept the biblical record of origins at face value, must deal with opponents from not one, but two different camps.

- First there are the strict evolutionists – men and women who retain no belief whatsoever in God or His Word. To them, their origin is strictly a naturalistic phenomenon – nothing more, nothing less.
- Second, there are the opponents who profess a belief in God and His Word, but who have compromised the biblical account of origins so that many aspects of the evolutionary cosmogony may be incorporated into that divine record.

If the theistic evolutionists, progressive creationists, and their cohorts are correct, we who have understood the biblical record to be taken as a literal, historical account of our ultimate origin are wrong. So I believe it is imperative that we firmly defend the Genesis account of origins as being a literal, historical account of God's activity in the realm of creation. Christ, and His Old and New Testament writers, viewed it as such; therefore we are not only correct in following their example, but absolutely must do so.

Christians may not ignore, be apathetic toward, or casual about false teachers. The Scriptures speak plainly on this subject. It is wrong for Christians to allow false teachers and their erroneous doctrines to go unchallenged (2 John 9-11). To the Christians at Rome, Paul wrote, "Now I urge you, brethren, note those who cause divisions and offenses, contrary to the doctrine which you learned, and avoid them. For those who are such do not serve our Lord Jesus Christ, but their own belly, and by smooth words and flattering speech deceive the hearts of the simple" (Romans 16:17-18). Jude's exhortation was that we "contend earnestly for the faith which was once for all delivered to the saints" (Jude 3).

Those who step forward to compromise the plain teaching of the inspired Word of God need to know that their compromises will not go unchallenged or unanswered. From time to time, however, Christians may be afflicted with either an attitude of indifference, or spiritual myopia (shortsightedness). Both of these critically impair effectiveness in spreading the Gospel.

A Christian's attitude of indifference may result from any number of factors, including such things as a person's own spiritual weakness, downtrodden spirit, a lack of serious Bible study, etc. Spiritual myopia, on the other hand, is often the end-product of either not having an adequate understanding of the Gospel message itself, or not wishing to engage in the controversy that is sometimes necessary to propagate that message.

One such example of spiritual myopia afflicting some Christians today centers on the biblical teaching regarding origins. Because no one is particularly fond of either controversy or playing the part of the controversialist, it is not uncommon nowadays to hear someone say, "Why get involved in controversial 'peripheral' issues like creation and evolution? Just teach the Gospel." Or, one might hear it said that "since the Bible is not a textbook of science, and since it is the Rock of Ages which is important, and not the age of rocks, we should just 'preach Christ'."

- First, those who suggest that we not concern ourselves with "peripheral" topics such as creation and evolution, and that we instead "just preach the Gospel," fail to realize that the Gospel includes creation and excludes evolution.
- Second, those who advise us to simply "emphasize saving faith, not faith in creation," have apparently forgotten that the most magnificent chapter in all the Bible on the topic of faith (Hebrews 11) begins by stressing the importance of faith in the creation of all things by God (verse 3) as preliminary to any kind of meaningful faith in His promises.
- Third, in order to avoid the offense which may come from preaching the complete Gospel, some simply would regard creation as unimportant. God, however, considered it so important that it was the topic of His first revelation. The first chapter of Genesis is the very foundation of the rest of the biblical record. If the foundation is undermined, it will not be long until the superstructure built upon it collapses as well. Should the first chapters of the Bible prove untrustworthy, upon what basis would one conclude that those which follow merit any confidence?
- Fourth, many Christians today have overlooked the impact on their own faith of not teaching what God has said about creation. G. Richard Culp (an author) stated it well. "One who doubts the Genesis account will not be the same man he once was, for his attitude toward Holy Scripture has been eroded by false teaching. Genesis is repeatedly referred to in the New Testament, and it cannot be separated from the total Christian message."

Christ and His inspired writers spoke often on the topic of creation and its relevance. The first eleven chapters of Genesis, sometimes referred to as the "creation chapters," are an integral part of the biblical record. They are not warts or growths that may be shaved off, leaving the remainder intact. If these teachings turn out to be either mythical or incorrect, it impeaches not only their testimony, but that of the Lord as well, for He accepted them as both correct and reliable, and used them often as a basis for His instructions and commandments in the New Testament.

The teachings of Moses and Christ are inseparably linked. "For if you believed Moses, you would believe Me; for he wrote about Me. But if you do not believe his writings, how will you believe My words?"

Why is a correct understanding of origins so important? Simply put, the answer is this: "If there is no creation, there is nothing else. If there is no Creator, then there is no Savior either."

So it does matter what we believe. With the acceptance of any system of origins must come simultaneously an acknowledgment of the implications that accompany it. Acceptance of organic evolution, for example, implies that: (a) there is no Creator; (b) religion is merely an invention of "evolved" man; (c) naturalistic forces are responsible for all that we are and see; (d) man is a "naked ape"; (e) there is no objective standard for truth and thus no set rules or regulations for ethics and/or morals; and (f) when this life is over, we are "like Rover, dead all over."

Acceptance of the biblical doctrine of creation likewise has implications. It implies, for example, that: (a) there is an eternal Creator; (b) religion is God-ordained; (c) super-natural forces have been at work in the past and therefore nature is not "all there is"; (d) man is a special creation produced by God "in His image"; (e) there is an objective standard for truth which provides guidelines for man's ethical and moral conduct; and (f) after this life, there is another life yet to come.

Similarly, any attempt to merge the two systems of origins has implications as well. Some have suggested that there is not necessarily a dichotomy in the matter of origins—that evolution and creation need not be separate, distinct, and opposing world views but instead may be happily combined. It is my position that such a marriage is unwarranted, unsuccessful, unscriptural, and unworthy of any support from those who revere the Word of God as verbally inspired and authoritative in these matters.

One of the most respected evolutionists in America during the past five decades was the late George Gaylord Simpson – known affectionately among his colleagues as "Mr. Evolution," in his book, *This View of Life*, addressed the compromise position of theistic evolution. Speaking of three well-known men who attempted to defend theistic evolution, Dr. Simpson remarked:

> *...Three great men and great souls, and all have flatly failed in their quest. It is unlikely that others can succeed where they did not, and surely I know of none who has. The attempt to build an evolutionary theory mingling mysticism [Simpson's euphemism for creation] and science has only tended to vitiate the science. I strongly suspect that it has been equally damaging on the religious side.*

The loss of respect for the Bible as the inspired Word of God that eventually results from the acceptance of various creation compromises is utterly tragic.

Even more tragic, however, is the ultimate effect of such compromises on a person's faith. Sooner or later, the Bible-believer comes to realize that if the first eleven chapters of Genesis are not trustworthy, neither are those that follow.

Background Info on Genesis

Meaning: Origin or Beginning.

Writer: Moses

- "If it could be proved that Moses did not write the Pentateuch and that the Pentateuch is neither genuine nor authentic, the credibility of every other book of the Old Testament would be lost. Not only would the Old Testament books be seriously questioned, but even the words of our Savior would be rejected, for he attributed the authorship of the Pentateuch to Moses" (Pledge).
- There has been no valid evidence offered by critics which disproves Mosaic authorship of Genesis (and the Pentateuch). The author shows a thorough acquaintance with many matters pertaining to Egypt. He was familiar with many Egyptian names such as that of On, the native name for Heliopolis. Moses had the background for such knowledge. He was born, reared, and educated in Egypt; he had the opportunity and time to write the Pentateuch during the forty years of wandering in the wilderness.
- It should always be remembered that Moses was merely the human instrument through whom God chose to reveal the information recorded. The stories he recorded, the commands he spoke, and the precepts he uttered, all came from the Lord. The emphasis should not be placed on the human author, but upon the fact of his inspiration and the text itself.

Date:

- About 1400 B.C. The book covers about 2,500 years of history. This is more than half the time covered by the entire Old Testament.

Key Word:

- Beginning

Lesson for Today:

- All life came from God and is, therefore, responsible to Him now and in the judgment.

The Qualities of Genesis:

1. This is a book of history and without its important messages it would be difficult, if not impossible, to understand the rest of the Old Testament and most of the New Testament.
2. It has always been considered a great book in the literary world. It has been studied worldwide because of its literary qualities.
3. The supreme value of this great book is not literary nor historical, but religious. In it we discover the revelation of the only God who is infinitely wise, good and powerful. In it we are also told of God's relationship to the origin of the universe and His relationship to the history of many nations.
4. Genesis does not deal with imaginary heroes but with actual men and women with whom God had real communication and dealings. God not only showed them His grace and mercy, but revealed to them that He would bring a Redeemer who would be one of their descendants, and He would be a blessing to the whole world.

The Purposes of Genesis:

1. To reveal man's beginning and the history of his first acts.
2. To reveal God's promises to man and His providence in carrying out those promises.
3. The providence and promises of God are clearly visible in the book of Genesis.
4. 12 tribes to nations – To become a nation requires a law, a land, the ruled, and a ruler.
5. Genesis gives a brief survey of divine history from the beginning until Israel enters Egypt. The book is not intended to give a complete and detailed account of history, but rather a survey of significant events and people relating to God's plan to redeem man.
6. "The circumstances that precisely give the information needed to make the book of Exodus intelligible is supplied by the book of Genesis. It is in Genesis that the promises to Abraham, Isaac, and Jacob are spelled out ... Moreover, the fact that Exodus 1:1 begins with 'and' (Hebrew) indicates that it was intended to follow some preceding book" (Gleason Archer, Jr., p.169).

* It is important as we study the Bible to remember that the chapter and verse breaks were placed my man, not God.

Genesis – The Book Of Beginnings

The Universe --- 1:1-25
Man and Woman -- 1:26-2:25
Sin and Death --- 3:1-7
The Redemptive Promise -- 3:8-24
Sacrifice -- 4:1-15
Civilization -- 4:16-9-29
Diverse Languages and Nations -- Ch. 10-11
The Jewish Nation through Whom the Messiah Would Come ----------- Ch. 12-50

Genesis – Chapter 1

The History of Creation

Read Genesis 1.

1) When we talk about creation, we are talking about bringing something out of nothing.

Science says that there are four things required for creation. Everything that science says in involved in creation is present here. Remember, true science and God's word are always compatible.

1. Time   -   In the beginning,
2. Energy   -   God created,
3. Space   -   Heaven and,
4. Material   -   Earth.

This shows at least five attributes of God:

1. Eternity – God is eternal. God has no beginning and no end. God IS.
2. Immensity – Within God is all of creation. Earth, stars, galaxies, as far as you want to go. We cannot comprehend it.
3. Omnipotence – Having all power to do anything that is the object of power; and having lost no power in accomplishing it.
4. Omniscience – All knowledge of everything that is the object of knowledge; past, present, future, real or imaginary.
5. Omnipresence – Present everywhere that is an object of presence, and yet, it doesn't contain Him. Some religious groups will have you believe that God is in the trees, animals, etc. Wrong! All of these are in God.

*This is all shown in the creation.

The Hebrew word here for God is Elohim. The <u>im</u> at the end is the equivalent of our '<u>s</u>' in English. This is a plural word and it is used with a singular verb. This is the Hebrew equivalent to our word Godhead.

There is only one essence of deity, but there are three persons (or personalities) within that essence; the Father, the Son, and the Holy Spirit. Read Deuteronomy 6:4. The word "one" used in that verse is the Hebrew *echad*, which means "properly united, that is, one." It is a numeral from the Hebrew word *achad*, which means "to unify." With that understanding, we can conclude that the Lord our God is a <u>combined one</u>.

2-5) The 1st Day – Light and dark – As we mentioned, there are some who will tell us that each day represents a "long period of time." Scripture does not agree. Exodus 20:11 – Moses says it took 6 days.

2) *The Earth* – This is the main point of this narrative. The heavens are no longer considered, and their creation process is unimportant to Moses' message. This style is seen throughout the Bible.

Think of Abraham. Abraham had many descendants, but Scripture narrows the focus down to Isaac. And so on.

Without form, and void – In its original shape, not as a destroyed earth to be reshaped again. It was empty and formless.

And the Spirit of God was hovering over the face of the waters – This is the Holy Spirit. Among other things, He garnished the heavens during creation. Job 26:13 clarifies the Holy Spirit's work in creation.

3) *Then God said* – His Word created – His Word is Christ! (cf. Hebrews 11:3; John 1:1-4)

Let there be light; and there was light – Notice there is light but no sun. God created light in transit. God created the light before the sun and the moon. This will come into play a little later.

God spoke the word, and it was done. Could any process of creating light gradually even be imagined? Any chain of events leading to the development of light is inconceivable, the very thought of such a thing being rejected by the intelligence. Primeval darkness demands just the command revealed in this verse as the only possible solution for it.

4) *And it was good* – All of God's works are good and perfect for the purpose that He does them. There is no:

- Trying and testing
- Experimentation as with an unskilled craftsman – We talked about God's omniscience.

He is all knowing. He knows everything that is a possibility. He knows what perfection takes. He speaks it and it is done. Compare Isaiah 55:11. God's word does what He sends it out to do.

*God spoke it, it was done and it was good.

6-8) The 2nd Day – Firmament = expanse.

The creation of the earth's atmosphere was God's work on the second day of creation. One scholar pointed out that the term "firmament" carries the meaning of "an expanse ... the beating out as of a plate of metal." This suggests the utility of a shield, an appropriate figure indeed when it is recalled that the earth would long ago have been destroyed by showers of meteorites had it not been for the protection of our atmosphere.

Under the firmament/above the firmament – Divided our atmosphere from the heavens. The outer space (above the firmament) is called heaven.

Divided the waters…from the waters – Water exists upon earth in both liquid and vapor forms, and it is precisely the atmosphere which separates these. Men should marvel indeed at this creation, when it is remembered that millions and billions of tons of water are constantly suspended in the atmosphere in the form of clouds; and of course being much heavier than the atmosphere, only an act of creation could have accomplished such a thing. The patriarch Job marveled at this wonder: "Do you know how the clouds are balanced, those wondrous works of Him who is perfect in knowledge?" – Job 37:16

9-13) The 3rd Day – Dry land and vegetation. The waters were gathered together – how? Read Psalm 104:5-9.

One who examines a global map of the earth will see that the oceans are all connected literally, in "one place." And yet a division among the seas is inherent in the very word "seas" (plural). There can be no adequate explanation of this accuracy apart from understanding it as inspired of God. Neither Moses, nor any other writer of that ancient time, had any personal knowledge that could have led to such a statement.

Vegetation <u>according to its kind</u>. The earth to bring forth grass, herbs, and trees. These then bring forth seed. The adult came first!

* The answer to the chicken and egg question!

** I still don't know if Adam had a belly button.

*** Adam would have looked like an adult. But his age at his creation was 1 day.

Here is the law that like produces like. This eternal law of God regarding life yielding seed "after their kind" has never been repealed.

14-19) The 4th Day – Sun, moon, and stars. There are two greater lights – the Sun and Moon. The light was previously created, but these were added to give us day and night. They were also added to give us seasons.

15) *To give light on the earth* – This shows that from this point on our light is to be received from these. Light from these sources takes time to get to earth. This takes us back to day one. God, on day one, created "light in transit." When the star was made, the light was already coming to the earth. It then continues to come from the star. Remember, we are dealing with God! He is not bound like we are. We covered His characteristics earlier.

20-23) The 5th Day – Sea animals and birds.

20) *Let the waters abound* – This is not the same Hebrew word as in verse 11. There the earth brought forth from its elements. Here it means "swarm with swarms," e.g. schools of fish.

21) *God created great sea creatures* – "Sea creatures of great length." This shows that there was no transmutation of species, each was created by God.

22) *And God blessed them, saying, be fruitful and multiply* – God's blessing was the power to be fruitful and to multiply.

24-31) The 6th Day – Living creatures (cattle, etc.) and man.

Again: <u>Let the earth bring forth</u>:

   a. Cattle – domestic animals,
   b. Creeping things – smaller creatures and
   c. Beasts – wild animals.

26) *Then God said, "Let Us make man in Our image, according to Our likeness"* – God… US … Our … Our – Plural. All three members of the Godhead are involved in the creation:

   a. Father – here in v. 26
   b. Son – John 1:1-4; Hebrews 1:3
   c. Holy Spirit – v.2

*One essence of Deity – Three personalities in that one essence. All three cooperate in everything that is done.

Our image…Our likeness – Man, unlike animals, is an eternal spirit with the ability to recognize (by our own free will) that we need to do better in order to be right with God. It is also significant that man himself is a trinity – having mind, spirit, and body. Other phases of human likeness to God are seen in such things as moral responsibility, intellectual achievement, and creativity.

27) *In the image of God…He created them* – This means that woman also is made in the image of God.

28) *God blessed them …be fruitful …multiply …fill* – Again, God's blessing includes the power to multiply, but it is also delivered as a command. Here we have the institution of marriage between man and woman.

31) *And indeed, it was very good* – Seventh time – see verses 4, 10, 12, 18, 21 and 25 all "good." But here it is "very good." There were absolutely no imperfections in God's creation – it was "very good!" Evolution teaches that things had to be "perfected" as time went on through the evolutionary process.

It is clear in this six-day sequence that the progress of God's creative activity was upward toward man. In fact, the special thrust of this entire creation narrative is pointed squarely at the emergence of man upon earth as the crowning act of all creation!

It is important to note here that God did not create evil! It was introduced into the world later. The only way God could have insured that there would be no evil would be to have created other perfect gods or created robots with no will of their own. The mere fact that God's creatures are less than perfect gods or less than perfect robots gives occasion for those creatures to choose to go against God's will (in other words, sin).

Genesis – Chapter 2

The History of Creation – Continued

Intro) This chapter is a further elaboration of the revelation of God regarding the creation. It is most logical and fully in keeping with the unity of the entire book to find here in Genesis 2 an elaboration of what was revealed in Genesis 1.

This chapter is not another and contradictory account of creation, but a review of certain phases of creation, with respect to a new focus of interest, namely that of humanity. It must be viewed as supplementary information to what is already revealed in the preceding chapter.

Read Genesis 2:1-7.

1-3) The 7th Day – God rested (from creation).

2) *God ended His work which He had done* – Creation is finished. The laws of nature are set into motion and all is complete.

3) *He rested from all His work which God had created and made* – God declared to be finished with His creative work. This does not mean that God ceased working altogether. This is also not the Sabbath rest that will be given to the Jews centuries later.

Rested – Literally: "ceased" or "desisted."

Note: This is a Sabbath from creation for God. Not the Jewish Sabbath for men! (cf. Ex 20:8-10). All efforts to associate the creation Sabbath with the Jewish Sabbath should be resisted. There is no indication whatever that Adam ever heard of a Sabbath. The Sabbath was made known, not to Adam, but to Moses (Nehemiah 9:13-14); and the reason for the Jewish observance of the Sabbath given to them was not because God rested on the creation Sabbath, but "the deliverance of Israel from slavery in Egypt" (Deuteronomy 5:15). The Sabbath was never a sign between God and all men, but, "It is a sign between me (God) and the children of Israel" (Exodus 31:17).

Some notable scholars claim that this period of rest is still going on. They reference Hebrews 4:4-6, 11 to back this claim. The idea is that this rest will continue until the final judgment.

4-6) *History* – The account of, proceedings, course of history.

These verses refer to a past time in creation, particularly the third day, before vegetation with fruit-bearing trees appeared. Just as Genesis 2:5-6 gave further details of the third day of creation, the next verses provide further information regarding the work of the sixth day in the creation of mankind.

7) This truth is perpetually attested in the fact that man's body returns to dust upon his death. "Earth to earth, dust to dust."

And breathed into his nostrils the breath of life – The special blessing of humanity is indicated, because none of the animals were given this special opportunity. Here is the impassable gulf that separates the animal kingdom from that of man. A special endowment was given to men. He became a living soul.

Life In God's Garden

Read Genesis 2:8-25.

9) The Tree of Life would have served its purpose (3:22) if man had won the upcoming trial and not eaten from the tree of the knowledge of good and evil. Its existence shows God had made ample provision for man's good. If Adam and Eve would have not yielded to temptation they would have remained in the garden forever. But they failed the test and lost the tree of life.

That some type of symbolism is involved in understanding the trees is clear. The disaster to Adam and Eve did not come from the fruit of the forbidden tree, but from their eating of it in violation of the commandment of God.

The necessity of two trees to deliver the entire truth to mankind appears in the fact that man's eating of the forbidden tree also resulted in the loss of the other tree. Inherent in this is the truth that, if man had obeyed his Creator, death would not have overtaken him, a deduction from the fact that the penalty was imposed after disobedience, with the inclusion of the idea that the penalty would not have been enforced apart from disobedience.

10-14) No exact location can be assigned as Eden; but our text makes it clear that it was a most desirable and beautiful home for mankind.

15) The ideal state of man was not one of idleness, but one of labor and responsibility. God gave Adam work before the fall! Work was not a punishment.

16, 19) Adam had a vocabulary when he was created. This vocabulary was extensive. He was able to understand what God was talking to him about, and was able to communicate back. Adam was also able to name all of these animals. This shows that we did not have to develop language over many years.

17) *Shall not eat* – this is emphatic. Even better, "must not." This is a command! Every line of this chapter moved straight to the climactic revelation here, this divine commandment.

Shall surely die – Dying is separation from God. This separation occurred the second they broke God's law. And physical death closes the experience if repentance and obedience do not come first (cf. 2 Corinthians 7:10). This account definitely teaches that man was created with "free will" or "free moral agency."

Man died spiritually the moment sin entered the scene. Man was separated from God. Physical death also entered the scene. It took a few centuries, in Adam's case, but look at our short lives now.

18) *It is not good that man should be alone* – Man in the state of being alone is incomplete, unfulfilled, and lacking in much that he was created to be. This law has never been repealed.

A helper comparable to him – Lit: "like him" as agreeing with him in nature; his counterpart.

She is the kind of help man needs, agreeing with him:

   a. Mentally
   b. Physically
   c. Spiritually

* This was not to be found in all the other animals God brought to him.

** She is not an inferior being! There will be set a "chain of command." This does not mean that one is inferior to the other. The N.T. lays out a ruling order: God, Christ, Man, then woman. Christ is not inferior to God. Woman is not inferior to man. They both make us the unit.

21-22) There is a great type/anti-type relationship introduced in God's revelation here. The sleep coming upon Adam is a type of the death of Christ on Calvary; and just as the wife of Adam was taken from his side during that sleep, so the Church of Jesus Christ, the Bride of Christ was, in a figure, taken from the side of Jesus, from which, upon its being pierced by the spear, there came forth blood and water, emblematical of the two grand ordinances of Christianity, namely, the Lord's Supper and Christian baptism.

Why the rib? As many have noted, woman was taken not from Adam's foot that he might rule over her, not from Adam's head that she might dominate him, but from his side that she might be his true equal and companion. It is also worth noting that ribs can regenerate. I must also mention that men and women both have 12 pairs of ribs. There have been religious folks in the past who have claimed that since Eve was taken from Adam's rib, men have less ribs than women. This is not true.

Is this account historical? Yes! The history of the whole race of mankind begins right here in this chapter; and concerning the first chapter in that history, this is the only record that man has. Paul understood this record as straightforward history, observing that man was not made from woman, but woman from man (1 Corinthians 11:8).

Now look at 1 Corinthians 11:12… The woman was out of the man. The man is through (or by means of) the woman. How do men come today? Through birth, through a woman. But all things are out of God. This matches the Genesis account exactly! There are no contradictions in Scripture!

24) *They shall become one flesh* – This is the same word (one) we mentioned before that means "a combined one," a "unit." The man and woman became a combined unit.

Our Lord quoted from both chapter 1 and 2 of Genesis in a single breath (Matthew 19:4-6), linking Genesis 1:27 and Genesis 2:24 as both being attributable to God Himself. These passages tied together are the basis of Jesus' moral standard concerning marriage and His condemnation of divorce.

25) This is a glimpse of the innocence that belonged to man before the entrance of sin into His Paradise.

The Days of Creation

First Day ----------------------------------- Light and Dark
Second Day ------------------------- Firmament (Expanse)
Third Day ---------------------------- Dry Land and Plants
Fourth Day-------------------------- Sun, Moon, and Stars
Fifth Day -------------------------- Sea Animals and Birds
Sixth Day ------------------------- Land Animals and Man
Seventh Day ------------------- God Rested From Creation

1. A Biblical statement or word is to be taken as literal unless there is something in the context which demands that it be taken as a figure of speech. There is nothing in the local or general context which indicates these days are not literal days.
2. The days are equally divided between light and darkness. Plants were created on the third day; if the days were long geological periods, these plants would have died due to the extremely long and cold nights; the deep cold would be caused by the absence of sunlight for that long period of darkness. Also, many plants depend on insects to propagate; but insects were not created until the sixth day. Even if these days were only a few years in length, this plant life would have perished.
3. The word "day" is translated from the Hebrew *yom*. This Hebrew word is used figuratively to refer to longer periods of time than the literal 24-hour day in many instances. However, in all instances where it is used with a numerical prefix, it always has reference to a literal solar day. In Genesis one, the numeric values of first, second, etc., are used. There are more than 100 such usages in the Old Testament. Moreover, when the plural form of "yom" is used, it always refers to 24-hour days. There are more than 700 such usages of the word in the Old Testament.
4. In the context, the seventh day is not distinguished from the other six days in length. We have no reason to believe it was any longer or shorter than the others. "For in six days the LORD made heaven and earth, the sea, and all that in them is, and rested the seventh day: wherefore the LORD blessed the sabbath day, and hallowed it" (Exodus 20:11). Adam and Eve were created on the sixth day. If the days were long geological periods of the length modernists claim, then Adam was extremely old before day number six ended. He lived through part of day six, through all of day seven, and for the rest of his 930 years. If these days were long eons of time, Adam would have been far older than the age assigned him. Many are unwilling to give up their day-age interpretation of Genesis one, and so have been driven to assert that Adam was not a real person. But New Testament passages clearly affirm that Adam was a real man, and the first man.

- a. Matthew 19:4: "And he answered and said unto them, Have ye not read, that he which made them at the beginning made them male and female."
- b. 1 Corinthians 15:21-22, 47: "For since by man came death, by man came also the resurrection of the dead. For as in Adam all die, even so in Christ shall all be made alive ... The first man is of the earth, earthy: the second man is the Lord from heaven."

5. The Hebrew word "yom" is used and defined in Genesis 1:5: "And God called the light Day, and the darkness he called Night. And the evening and the morning were the first day."
   - a. "As added proof, the word is clearly defined the first time it is used. God defines his terms! 'And God called the light Day, and the darkness he called Night. And the evening and the morning were the first day' (Genesis 1:5). Yom is defined here as the light period in the regular succession of light and darkness, which, as the earth rotates on its axis, has continued ever since. This definition obviously precludes any possible interpretation as a geologic age" (Whitcomb).
   - b. b. God plainly said "the evening and morning were the first day." Genesis 1:14 says that the sun and moon were to divide the day from the night, that they were to be for signs, seasons, days, and for years. If the "days" were ages, then what are the years? What is the night?

6. "Had Moses wanted us to understand that these 'days' were actually long, geological periods of time, he could have used words that so specified this point. But he did not! He could have used the Hebrew word 'olam,' or the word 'dor,' both of which would indicate indefinite periods of time. He could have modified the Hebrew 'yom' by the adjective 'rab' (yom rab—a 'long' day), but again, he did not. As one author has correctly pointed out, if God said that he created everything in six days, but really used six eons, wouldn't that make God a deceptive, tricky, sneaky, deceitful God?" (Thompson, p.10).

Genesis – Chapter 3

The Temptation and Fall of Man

Intro) This chapter details the temptation and fall of humanity and their consequent expulsion from Eden. The tempter is introduced (Genesis 3:1); the temptation is presented (3:2-5); the fall of Eve, then Adam, (3:6); the consequent shame, loneliness, and fear (3:7-8); their confrontation with God and their futile excuses (3:9-13); the curse of the serpent and the word of hope for mankind (3:14-15); the outline of the penalties upon Eve and Adam (3:16-20); and their expulsion from Eden (3:21-24) are other developments that bring the chapter to its conclusion.

Read Genesis 3.

1) What was the serpent prior to the curse? Was it a member of the animal kingdom or was it not? It is not stated that the serpent was more cunning than any <u>other</u> beast of the field, but that he was more cunning than any beast. This may be an indication that he was not a beast at all prior to the curse. Whatever the serpent was, he was endowed with the ability to speak.

Of course, the whole person of the serpent that appears in this tragic scene also includes a certain identity with Satan himself, as indicated by Paul's reference in 2 Corinthians 11:3, the indication there being that the same serpent who seduced Eve is, in this dispensation, engaged in seducing the Church of Jesus Christ. Also, Satan is called, "The great Dragon, the old serpent, he that is called the Devil and Satan, the deceiver of the whole world" (Revelation 12:9).

Has God indeed said – Satan's first attack is against the word of God! Satan must attack God's word in order to discredit it.

Satan's approach is to get Eve (and us) to doubt what God has said. If Satan can get Eve to not believe what God has said, he can get Eve to disobey what God has said. In this respect, this temptation is a type of all temptation, for the very opposite of belief is disobedience. Look at John 3:36… Unfortunately, the KJV and the NKJV don't translate this quite well enough. The ASV, NASV and ESV do. The Greek word translated "does not believe" in John 3:36 is best translated "is not subject to." The definitions given for the word are as follows: To be disobedient, refuse compliance; Disobey, rebel, be disloyal, refuse conformity; To disbelieve (willfully and perversely); Not to allow one's self to be persuaded; To refuse belief and obedience.

4) Satan quotes God here but adds the word "not." Again, this is a type of what we face today. Satan is very crafty. But, we must hold to the word of God, the standard for our lives. (cf. Revelation 22:18; Deuteronomy 4:2; 12:32; Proverbs 30:6).

5-6) Satan presents all avenues of temptation. He does not want to fail!

Compare Eve's temptation with 1 John 2:16:
- Food – lust of the flesh

- Pleasant to the eye – lust of the eye
- Will be like God – pride of life

Satan, as we'll see, was successful with causing the fall of man by appealing to these lusts. So, why not try it with the Son of God (Matthew 4)?

- Bread – lust of the flesh
- All He could see – lust of the eye
- Jump (God would not allow any harm to come to His Son) – pride of life.

6) *She also gave to her husband with her, and he ate* – Adam failed to restrict her, allowed this sin and is therefore responsible to God for this failure even though he was not the one who was deceived (1 Timothy 2:14). Thus, Adam sinned deliberately with his eyes wide open, whereas Eve was deceived.

7) *Eyes opened* – knew. They eat and expect marvelous results, they wait and there grows within them the sense of shame. Satan has his victory.

8) *Adam and his wife hid themselves from the presence of the Lord* – It was impossible, of course, for the sinful couple to hide from the Creator, but that did not prevent their trying to do so. Men still try to hide from God by turning away from Bible reading, forsaking worship services, and by pretending to be so busy that they have no time for thoughts of God.

10-11) There was no way for Adam to hide his sinful condition from God. The mention of his nakedness and his hiding laid bare his ugly secret. God, even before the foundation of the world, and before Adam and Eve had been created and placed in Eden, had anticipated their sin and had formulated the remedy for their transgression. God went straight to the heart of the problem and asked Adam if he had eaten of the forbidden fruit.

12-13) Adam's response was weak and insufficient. Instead of confessing the sin he had committed, he gave excuses, even to the effect that maybe God Himself was to blame, for He had given to Adam the woman who had given the fruit of the tree, so what else was there for Adam to do but to eat!

In Eve's reply, there is the same fault that marred the response of Adam – no admission of sin, no asking of pardon, no expression of regret or sorrow, but merely a weak maneuver to place the blame upon the serpent who had "deceived" her!

15) First Messianic prophecy (cf. John 8:44; Galatians 4:4; Hebrews 2:14; 1 John 3:8; Romans 16:20).

He shall bruise your head – This is a promise of ultimate and complete victory over evil by the Lord Jesus Christ. This, of course, took place on Calvary, where Christ slew him "who had the power of death" (Hebrews 2:14).

16) *I will greatly multiply your sorrow and your conception; in pain you shall bring forth children* – The frightful pangs of childbirth do not appear in nature in similar situations in the lower creation, and they are a continual reminder to all men of the fallen estate of the race.

17) More difficult work now. This is because he submitted to his wife, instead of ruling the situation. He shall experience insubordination on the part of the soil, where otherwise he would have experienced complete control.

20) Eve. Means "Life" or "Living." This verse has the utility of emphasizing that Adam and Eve were the first humans on earth, and that all subsequent generations of the human family descended from them, a fact also inherent in the apostolic injunction that God "made of one," all the families of men to dwell on the earth (Acts 17:26).

21) Tunics (coats) of skins. Fig leaves were not enough (cf. 1 Timothy 2:9). Our nakedness is not to be flaunted or displayed for the world.

You notice that God used the skins of animals to cover Adam and Eve. People today, even in the church, don't like to wear anything that led to the death of an animal. Many vegetarians today (not all of them) say that we should not kill the animals. God placed these creatures on earth to sustain man!

22) The tragedy here is that Adam and Eve already knew that which was good and evil – all of this was to become like God.

It would have been an unqualified disaster if man had eaten of the tree of life and in consequence thereof lived forever in his shameful and humiliating condition. What man had already done was bad enough, but to prevent an even greater tragedy, God drove him out of the Paradise of Eden for man's sake.

The tree of life is nowhere explained in the Bible, but it disappears from the pages of the Bible here and never reappears until the closing chapters of the Book of Revelation, where once more, it is presented as growing on either side of the river of life, yielding its fruit twelve seasons in the year, and the leaves of which are for the healing of the nations. Clearly, from what is said here, it is that reality which bestows immortality.

24) There will be no return to this garden on earth. We do not know how long the garden remained or even where it was. We may only lift up our hearts in prayer and thanksgiving to Almighty God who, through the gift of his Beloved Son, has made it possible for those who love him to enter once more into complete and loving fellowship with the Creator through Christ.

Satan's Victory and Defeat

His Victory		His Defeat
Adam	*Person Tempted*	Christ
Eden	*Place*	Wilderness
Without sin	*State*	Without Sin
Satan	*Tempter*	Satan
Disobedience	*Appeal*	Disobedience
Disobedience	*Action*	Obedience
Death	*Result*	Life

Sin the Conqueror	**Sin Conquered**
Genesis 3:1-8	Matthew 4:1-11

* Christ was able to withstand the temptations of Satan.

** Jesus Christ was 100% God and 100% man. His deity did not override His humanity.

*** Scripture says Jesus lived and presented Himself (miracles and wonders) by means of the Holy Spirit (Luke 4:1; John 3:34; Matthew 12:25-28).

**** Jesus was tempted just as we are (Hebrews 4:15). If His deity overrode His humanity, He wasn't tempted. There is no way He could be.

Genesis – Chapter 4

Cain Murders Abel

Intro) This chapter details the tragic story of two brothers, Cain and Abel, in whose lives there appeared a dramatic acceleration of the disastrous consequences of the Fall, just related in the preceding chapter.

In no way can we accept the assertion that this story is merely a myth. Jesus Christ himself referred to Abel as a "righteous man" (Matthew 23:35; Luke 11:50); and both Cain and Abel are repeatedly referred to in the N.T. as real characters, as in Hebrews 11:4, 12:24; 1 John 3:12; and Jude 11.

Read Genesis 4:1-15.

2) It should be particularly noted that nothing in this chapter indicates either that Cain was the firstborn of Adam and Eve, or that these two were the only children they had. Adam and Eve lived many centuries and had "sons and daughters" (Genesis 5:4); and the total number of their children could well have been fantastic.

3) *In process of time ...* – is an expression that moves this episode to a point long after the events of the preceding chapter.

4-5) A standard had been set! Read Hebrews 11:4; Romans 10:17. Nothing in the text indicated that this is the first sacrifice ever made. Faith comes by hearing the word of God. God had given the standard, and measured their gifts according to that standard. Sin is the result when we ignore the standard.

Thus, the great sin of Cain was simply this – he offered to God what he supposed would be just as good as what God commanded. Cain might have tried to justify his action. In modern terms, he may have said:

If God wants smoke, my haystack has that fuzzy lamb beat a hundred ways.
If God wants value, my wheat will buy fifty lambs.
And all that messy blood; I never liked that anyway!
God can save us if we never go near a drop of blood.
Surely, God doesn't care about a thing like that;
It's the spirit of the thing that counts anyway!

6) *Why has your countenance fallen?* – As in the case of God's asking Adam, "Where are you?" the Lord was not asking for information but to elicit a response from Cain whose anger flared up instantly. The fallen countenance is still the result of sin and guilt.

7) Man can win over temptation. If we look for a way of escape, God will provide it. "No temptation has overtaken you except such as is common to man; but God is faithful, who will not allow you to be tempted beyond what you are able, but with the temptation will also make the way of escape, that you may be able to bear it" (1 Corinthians 10:13).

9) *Am I my brother's keeper* – What a brutal and selfish response was this! All men are obligated to one another, and no man has the right to seek his own selfish ends without regard to what the effect may be upon others.

"Abel ... he being dead still speaks" (Hebrews 11:4).

What does the blood of Abel say?

1. The blood of Abel says that God will one day avenge the crimes perpetrated against the innocent (Romans 12:19).
2. The blood of Abel says that the righteous are hated without cause (1 John 3:11-13).
3. The blood of Abel says that it DOES make a difference how men worship Almighty God.
4. The blood of Abel says that faith is the only key to winning approval of God (Hebrews 11:6).
5. The blood of Abel says that the only righteousness is in obeying the Word of the Lord (Romans 1:16-17).

11-12) God's curses so far:

1. The serpent 3:14
2. The ground 3:17
3. Now a man

13-14) Cain is not sorry for his sin; it is the punishment he cannot bear (cf. 2 Corinthians 7:9-10). Cain heard his punishment and knew he could not escape it. Murderers fear they in turn will be slain by others.

Things we can learn from Cain and Abel.

1. God wants our best – Abel gave it. Cain did not, according to the standard.
2. God warns and offers a way of escape – Sin (Satan) is crouching in wait for you, but you can defeat it.
3. Our deeds are an outward physical statement of our inward thoughts.
4. Sin finds us out.
5. Punishment ≠ Repentance.
6. Our worth is not determined by the world.

The Family of Cain

Read Genesis 4:16-24.

16) *Nod* – The geographical location of this place is not known. The word means "wandering," and is apparently derived from the nomadic and fugitive life to which Cain was condemned

17) "City" need not be one as we know it. It could be just a very few houses and possibly some fence around for protection.

23-24) Here we have a boastful poem (1st poetry in the Bible). Lamech is giving the poem.

<u>Avenged</u> by Lamech himself (cf. Proverbs 20:22; Romans 12:17-21).

A New Son

Read Genesis 4:25-26.

25) Seth = Compensation, substituted.

26) This is public worship. Private worship had already been followed.

Genesis – Chapter 5

The Family of Adam

Intro) This remarkable chapter bridges the time-lapse between the Creation and the Flood. A couple items worth noting here in this chapter are: (1) the longevity of the antediluvian patriarchs, and (2) the chronology of the passage which gives us 1,656 years as the elapsed time between the Creation and the Great Deluge.

Read Genesis 5.

Names and ages of chapter 5:

1. Adam – 930
2. Seth – 912
3. Enosh – 905
4. Cainan – 910
5. Mahalaleel – 895
6. Jared – 962
7. Enoch – 365 – Rewarded with a shorter life and brought into eternity sooner.
8. Methuselah – 969
9. Lamech – 777
10. Noah – 950

There is nothing actually unreasonable about the extremely long lives of men in the morning of the race, before ravages of sin and disease had brought about the deterioration of men's bodies. Many scholars use the separation from the tree of life as a reason for the decline of age as time passes.

Had sons and daughters – This expression in Genesis 5:4, 7, 10, 13, 15, 19, 22, 26, 30, regarding all ten on the list (except Noah) indicates the stripped down nature of the genealogy. The naming of any individual was for the special purpose of establishing the line of Noah back to Adam. Most of the sons and all of the daughters were omitted. How many children did each have? The number could have been truly fantastic. No doubt there were many children born to each of these patriarchs besides the particular son who was designated. Only those who were destined to appear in the Messianic lines were singled out for identification.

24) *Enoch walked with God* – One scholar has pointed out that, due to the text, it seems it was "after he begot Methuselah," that Enoch walked with God. This may suggest that prior to that event he had not done so. Many a man has held his little son in his arms and resolved to follow a godly life, and it may be supposed that Enoch did the same thing. In any case, he was the most successful righteous man of all antiquity, because it is said that, "He was not, because God took him," also, that "Enoch walked with God."

The word signifies intimate companionship, and here denotes a fellowship with God morally and religiously perfect. Based upon the expression, "He was not, for God took him," we are to conclude that Enoch never died, but was translated into an eternal fellowship with the Creator. "By faith Enoch was taken away so that he did not see death" (Hebrews 11:5).

This chapter is preliminary to the account of the Deluge which was God's punishment upon rebellious mankind, but significantly, God was preparing a new beginning already present in the posterity of Noah.

The significance of the two divergent lines of the Cainites and the Sethites will appear at once in the following chapter. The Cainites grew progressively worse and worse, resulting in the judicial hardening of the entire race. The corruption could not be contained in the line of the Cainites but through their intermarriage with the Sethites, practically the whole of humanity came to be in total rebellion against Almighty God.

Genesis – Chapter 6

The Wickedness and Judgment of Man

Intro) This is one of the most significant chapters in the Bible, as evidenced by the N.T. references to it.

1. "The Divine longsuffering waited in the days of Noah, while the ark was being prepared, in which a few, that is, eight souls, were saved through water" (1 Peter 3:20).
2. "For this they willfully forget: that by the word of God the heavens were of old, and the earth standing out of water and in the water, by which the world that then existed perished, being flooded with water" (2 Peter 3:5-6).
3. "By faith Noah, being divinely warned of things not yet seen, moved with godly fear, prepared an ark for the saving of his household, by which he condemned the world and became heir of the righteousness which is according to faith" (Hebrews 11:7).
4. "But as the days of Noah were, so also will the coming of the Son of Man be. For as in the days before the flood, they were eating and drinking, marrying and giving in marriage, until the day that Noah entered the ark, and did not know until the flood came and took them all away, so also will the coming of the Son of Man be" (Matthew 24:37-39).

The historical truth of the event before us is categorically affirmed by the words of both Christ and his apostles. The universal, world-wide extent of it is a necessary deduction from the fact of Christ the Lord having made it a type of the universal and final judgment of humanity, and from the further fact of the apostle Peter's having made the salvation of Noah and his family "through water" a type of the salvation of the church through Christian baptism (1 Peter 3:21).

Analogies here regarding baptism:

1. It was the water of the flood that separated Noah from the disobedient nation that perished; and it is the water of Christian baptism that separates between the saved today and the disobedient who perish.
2. Noah's coming forth from the waters to live again on the earth might fitly be called his being "born of water."
3. The same waters which destroyed the ancient world were those which saved Noah by bearing up the ark and delivering him to newness of life. Just so, it is the water of baptism that destroys the wicked today, in the sense that they despise it, rebel against God's command, refuse to obey it; or, if they allow it at all, downgrade the necessity or importance of it.
4. Just as the water separated Noah from the past and delivered him to a new existence, it is the water of baptism that separates the Christian from his past and from which he like Noah, arises to "walk in newness of life."
5. The same element is instrumental in the salvation of Noah and that of the Christian, namely, water, exactly the same kind of water (whoever heard of different kinds of water?). It is not a spiritual baptism that saves men; it is water baptism, as the covenant act of obedience to the commandment of Almighty God.

6. It was the water that washed away the filth of that generation; and it is baptism that, in a figure, washes away the sins of men who are becoming Christians (Acts 22:16). "Arise, and be baptized, and wash away your sins."
7. Only a few were saved through the flood, and Christ has warned that only a few shall be saved (in the relative sense) unto eternal life (Matthew 7:13-14).
8. Note also that only those in the ark were saved, and that, similarly, only those in Christ (in the church) have the promise of eternal life.

Read Genesis 6:1-8.

1-3) *Sons of God* – I have heard people say that these were like angels of God who were going in and essentially raping these women. But we are dealing with righteous men, generally the line of Seth.

The reasons why this passage cannot be applied either to angels or to other supernatural creatures are as follows:

1. No angels have been mentioned in the Bible up to this point, and the supposition that they make their first appearance in Scripture under the title "sons of God" is untenable.
2. The term "sons of God" is nowhere in the Bible, either in the O.T. or in the N.T., applied to angels.
3. In the N.T., particularly, it is human beings who are led by God's Spirit who are called "sons of God" (1 John 3:1; Romans 8:14; Galatians 4:6, etc.).
4. There are only two classes of angels, the holy angels, and the angels of Satan (fallen angels); and neither class could be in view here. Holy angels would not have induced men to sin; and the fallen angels, in a million years, would never have been designated by the Holy Spirit as "the sons of God"!
5. Note too that these "sons of God" "took them wives of all that they chose," an unmistakable reference to marriage; and Jesus our Lord flatly declared that angels do not marry (Matthew 22:30).
6. If angels, or other supernatural creatures, had been to blame for the gross wickedness about to envelop mankind, then God would have announced *their* punishment and destruction, instead of the punishment and destruction of men.
7. The two classes of men visible in these verses had already been carefully introduced in Genesis 4 and Genesis 5, the sons of men (in their hardened state) being the line of the Cainites, and the "sons of God" being the people in the line of Seth.

Daughters of men – This is generally the line of Cain. The sons of God are beginning to look only on the external in order to choose wives.

An end must come. There will be judgment. But there will be a period of 120 years.

3) This signals the withdrawal of the Holy Spirit from those who already had hardened their hearts against God, and we find in this the first Scriptural instance of Judicial Hardening, a phenomenon witnessed again and again throughout the Bible.

4) *Giants* – Bullies, tyrants, attackers.

We do not have angels marrying human women! Compare; "For in the resurrection they neither marry nor are given in marriage, but are like angels of God in heaven" (Matthew 22:30).

5) It would be difficult to devise a sentence that would any more effectively portray the corruption of humanity than does Genesis 6:5.

6) *Was sorry* (repented) – Suffer grief, regret, avenge oneself. Henry says, "This is God's resentment of man's wickedness. He did not see it as an unconcerned spectator, but as one injured and affronted by it. He saw it as a tender father sees the folly and stubbornness of a rebellious and disobedient child, which not only angers him, but grieves him and makes him wish he had been written childless."

Another scholar said, "What is meant here is that God in consistency with His immutability assumes a changed position in respect to changed man. This cannot refer to any change in God; for as Malachi put it, 'I, Jehovah, change not'" (Malachi 3:6).

8) *Noah found grace in the eyes of the Lord* – It is not to be concluded that Noah was sinless, a quality that never pertained to anyone other than the Son of God himself. Nevertheless, as explained in the following verses, Noah was clearly apart from the universal corruption that otherwise engulfed the whole of humanity.

Noah Pleases God

Read Genesis 6:9-12.

12) *For all flesh had corrupted their way on the earth* – Note that the wickedness and unrestrained lawlessness and violence that marked human conduct were the result of their own actions. They had corrupted their way. It was not, therefore, the result of intermarriages with superhuman beings that produced the debauchery of mankind; it was simply due to their willful choice of evil conduct.

The Ark Prepared

Read Genesis 6:13-22.

13) *Has come before me* – According to my judgment. As a judge in his court.

I will destroy them with the earth – Not only life, but the physical environment of the earth itself would be involved according to this. What is meant is that a catastrophic disturbance of the whole planet would precipitate detrimental changes in the earth itself (cf. 2 Peter 3:4).

14-16) It is impossible from this description for men to make a diagram or replica of the ark, only the overall dimensions being recounted here. Nevertheless, what we know of it is impressive enough.

14) *Ark* – Chest, box. The ark was not designed to sail, but merely to float.

15) Length – 450'
   Width – 75'
   Height – 45' = 1,518,750 cu. Ft.
   Three decks in all.
   1 boxcar (40' x 9' x 8') = 2,880 cu. Ft. 527 boxcars in size.

* These measurements are considering the cubit as 18in. or 1 ½ ft. Could be longer or shorter.

** God gave the dimensions and specifications for the ark. Noah was not a boat-engineer, and just as God later showed Moses the pattern for the tabernacle, so also here, God gave the pattern of that which saved Noah and his family.

*** There is no doubt that miracles were involved here. Scripture says that God brings the animals to Noah. These pairs come peaceably together. God shuts the door. God brings the flood. Miracles did happen.

18) *I will establish My covenant with you* – With Noah, God made a covenant! The necessity for this covenant derived from the fact that the promise of deliverance God had made to Eve (Genesis 3:15) was apparently about to be abrogated and canceled through the death of all mankind, as God had just announced. What about the Seed (singular) who would crush the head of the Serpent? This covenant was God's arrangement with Noah, whereby the Seed would be delivered through him and his posterity.

22) Noah DID!

* It is appropriate to think a moment about the stupendous nature of this man's faith in what God told him. Such a flood was a seeming impossibility. The N.T. reveals that Noah preached (guided by the Spirit of Christ) for some 120 years during which time he was preparing the ark, preaching to those people of his own generation who must have mocked and belittled him. How they must have hooted about that crazy old man and his building such a monster of a boat. How was he ever going to get 45,000 tons moved in one piece to the water?! What a fool they thought him to be! They thought they were condemning him. Actually, it was HE who condemned them (Hebrews 11:7).

Genesis – Chapter 7

The Great Flood

Read Genesis 7.

1) God tells Noah to <u>come</u> into the ark. This indicates the presence of God with Him.

I have seen that you are righteous before Me – Noah's righteousness before God consisted of two things – his faith and his obedience. Noah had already been obeying God for a full 120 years while the ark was in preparation, his obedience consisting of his construction of the ark according to the pattern that God gave him, and his continual preaching to the wicked generation who were his contemporaries. Now, compare this to our idea of faith and righteousness today.

2-3) I'm simply not dogmatic about the number of clean or unclean animals on the ark. There are different opinions as to the numbers.

4) It is stated here that this event occurred a full week prior to the beginning of the Deluge; and it must be reckoned as a true act of faith that Noah obeyed this injunction implicitly. It was one thing to build the ark, and quite another to enter it and live there a week without any sign whatever of the necessity for it. We are not told how his fellow mortals reacted to this, but human nature being what it is, it is a foregone certainty that such an action was met with all kinds of scornful mockery.

First rain. God speaks from absolute authority:

- As creator
- As being in perfect control of nature, etc.
- God names the exact time of the beginning and the exact time of the end of the rains.

5) Noah did according to all that the Lord commanded him (cf. Hebrews 11:7). God told him what kind of wood to get, how to pitch in between the joints, how many levels to build and the full size of the ark. Noah obeyed. God accepted the ark as Noah built it.

7-9) The animals are put in the ark by God (cf. vv. 13-16).

10-11) Two sources of water:

- Fountains of the deep
- Windows of heaven (rains).

11) *Fountains of the great deep were broken up* – Great upheavals – this would explain why there are sea fossils on the tops of the Alps and other mountains.

13-16) *And they went into the ark to Noah* – This emphasizes and makes definite the truth that Noah did not seek out and drive all of those creatures into the ark; they went in unto him. This is clearly an act of God, having nothing whatever to do with Noah's independent activity.

16) *And the Lord shut him in* – There may have been some of those souls to whom Noah preached so long and so faithfully for whom Noah still had hope that they would enter and be spared; and he would have found it difficult indeed to close the door of hope; but God spared him that act of sorrow by Himself sealing the gate of life. The day of grace was then over. The long deserved destruction of rebellious mankind would appear at once. So it is today. Man can neither open nor close the way of salvation, either for themselves or for others. "See, I have set before you an open door, and no one can shut it" (Revelation 3:24). Our Lord Jesus Christ is described as, "He who is holy, He who is true, "He who has the key of David, He who opens and no one shuts, and shuts and no one opens" (Revelation 3:7b).

12, 17) The flood was forty days coming upon the earth. The Hebrew shows this is the duration of its coming not its duration upon the earth!

18-20) "The water prevailed" is stated three times in these three verses. This emphasizes the power and extent of the flood. It shows the power of surging upheavals, torrential rains, and tidal waves. But God kept the ark from being destroyed!

All the high hills [mountains] ... were covered. NOTE: All! Not just some of the mountains. Mt. Ararat = 16,900', Himalayas = 29,000'+.

21-23) The extent of the destruction of the flood. All flesh = All in whose nostrils was the breath of life. This does not include fish.

```
Fowl -------------------------------- Birds
Cattle ---------------- Domestic Animals
Beasts -------------------- Wild Animals
Creeping Things ---------- Reptiles, etc.
Men ---------------------------- Humans
```

24) Prevailed = Were mighty, conquered.

Note: The Flood was too high and too long not to be universal (Genesis 7:19-20)! Why would Noah need an ark if a local flood? He could have been far away in 100 years. So could have anyone else. If local, what about the fire in 2 Peter 3:10-12 (cf: 2:5)? Luke says all men were destroyed – 17:27.

Genesis – Chapter 8

Noah's Deliverance

Intro) This chapter covers the abatement of the flood and Noah's exit from the ark.

Read Genesis 8:1-19.

1) Then God remembered Noah – Remember ≠ remember something forgotten.

Remember = Remembering with kindness, granting request, protecting and delivering (cf. 1 Samuel 1:11; Genesis 9:15-16; Exodus 2:24).

The loving pity of the Father is the only thing that prevented the total annihilation of mankind, and that merciful concern is evident in God's remembering Noah.

God made a wind to pass over the earth – Such a phenomenon would have had a dual effect of (1) evaporation, and of (2) substantially aiding the movement of vast quantities of water back into the depression created by shifting and settling of the land level under the seas. The amount of the waters visible in this narrative requires the understanding that some major shift in land and ocean levels occurred. Refer to 2 Peter 3:5-7.

2-5) The flood waters receded.

7-12) Testing of the earth by birds:
   a. Raven – would land anywhere – seven more days
   b. Dove – would land on a dry surface – seven more days
   c. Dove – success – olive leaf – seven more days
   d. Dove – did not return – dry land.

13-14) Duration of the flood – 1 year and 10 days (Genesis 7:11; 8:14).
v. 13 -waters gone (local outlook).
v. 14 -earth itself dry (global outlook)

15-19) God commands Noah (and the animals) to vacate the ark. These state simply that, in obedience to God's command, Noah, and all the creatures on the ark, after their families, went forth out of the ark.

God's Covenant with Creation

Read Genesis 8:20-22.

20-22) An offering of thanksgiving. Noah has just witnessed the destruction of all living things including mankind with the exception of those who are on the ark.

Such sacrifices were not first initiated by Moses, but were instituted from the fall of man.

God makes a promise to Noah:

    a. He will not curse the ground again although the imagination of man's heart is evil from his youth.
    b. He will not destroy every living thing (smite) "... as I have done" (cf. 2 Pet 3:5-7).
    c. While the earth remains: (1) Seed time and harvest, (2) Cold and heat, (3) Winter and summer, (4) Day and night, SHALL NOT CEASE!

21) *Although the imagination of man's heart is evil from his youth* – Noah and his descendants will not be any better than were the posterity of Adam. Despite such a fact, God would nevertheless go forward with his Operation Mankind. Rather than destroy the whole race again, God would find other means of reaping the intended harvest from the populations of earth. Those other means would include at a later time, the introduction of the device of the "Chosen People," and still later, the visitation of our world by the Glorious One, Jesus Christ our Lord.

As I have done – This clause is a qualifier of the whole passage. The simple meaning of it is that the Great Deluge will never be duplicated in the subsequent history of the world.

22) *While the earth remains* – This is not a promise that the established order will continue eternally, but that "as long as the earth itself exists," that order will continue.

The Scriptures make it explicit that there is still another event that shall annihilate the whole world in the fires of the eternal judgment (2 Peter 3). The same world that was destroyed in the Flood has yet another appointment on the "day of judgment and destruction of ungodly men."

Genesis – Chapter 9

God's Promise to Noah

Intro) This chapter has been referred to as the "Fall of Noah," others have suggested it might equally be called the "Second Fall of Mankind."

The most remarkable thing in the chapter is that the great hero of the Flood is here presented as a weak and sinful man.

Within this chapter we will also see the germ of civil government.

Read Genesis 9:1-17.

1) *Be fruitful and multiply, and fill the earth* – The same blessing as to Adam and Eve (1:28). God's blessings again included the power to multiply! It is recognition in Noah of a second forefather for the human race.

2) There seems to be revealed here some fundamental change in the human creation's relationship to the animal kingdom. Just what it is, I'm unable to say.

3-4) There is much difference of opinion about whether or not man had been permitted to eat meat before this, and my opinion is that nobody knows for sure. You can make decent arguments either way.

Prohibition against eating blood (cf. Lev 17:11). This would become a Jewish Law. Is it a Christian law as well (Acts 15:20)?

5-6) Prohibition against the taking of human life. Following the murder of his brother Abel, Cain's fear that someone would kill him (Genesis 4:14) shows that even he realized that his crime deserved death. Henceforth, the murderer would receive the retribution that his crime deserved. Capital punishment for murderers is a law here instituted by God Himself. The just application of such a law would necessitate the creation of a judiciary with power to exonerate those who were inadvertently guilty in a technical sense, but whose lives should be spared, as later formalized in the Law of Moses in the establishment of the cities of refuge. The germ of government is also in this.

By man his blood shall be shed – Vengeance is the Lord's – Romans 12:19. This is not merely a permission legalizing, but an imperative command enjoining capital punishment. Only God has the right to take life, but in this commandment, it is clear that, when God commands man to execute murderers, He delegates this task to him, and it becomes his God-given responsibility to do it. The repeal of capital punishment by many states today is not merely a mistake, it is a violation of God's law. This responsibility serves as a barrier against the supremacy of evil.

Under the patriarchal dispensation, the next of kin was given this responsibility, such an individual being called "the avenger of blood." In our own times the police authority of the central government is charged with the task, but in both instances, "The authorities that exist are appointed by God" (Romans 13:1).

Why should we ultimately leave judgment (for sins committed against us) up to the Lord?

a. I may judge too harsh – over punish.
b. I may not judge harsh enough.
c. I may judge based on bias or partiality.
d. God's knowledge is true. His punishment will match the sin.

8-17) The covenant of the rainbow:

a. *"By the waters of a flood..."* (11) This is the prime qualifier of this covenant. The promise was not that "never again would the earth be destroyed," but that it would not be done a second time by means of a flood. The N.T. is explicit, as also the Minor Prophets, that another total destruction of the earth will yet occur, by means of fire (2 Peter 3).
b. The rainbow is the sign! It is still with us!
c. *I will look on it to remember the everlasting covenant* – Remember with kindness, granting requests, protecting and delivering (cf.8:1).

This covenant is absolutely unconditional. So many covenants in the Scripture are conditional based upon obedience. Not this one!

Noah and His Sons

Read Genesis 9:18-29.

18-19) The following account of the fall of Noah is an extremely abbreviated one; and without this connection between Ham and Canaan, we would be unable to make certain connections in the story.

20-24) Noah becomes drunk, and he became (was) uncovered [uncovered himself].

Ham saw the nakedness – "with delight" and told [with delight] in the Hebrew. The idea is "with lightness and not with respect and solemnity." Anything but a reverent attitude! His brothers' attitudes were quite different.

25) Cursed be Canaan – We certainly see the aftermath of this (Hivites – Josh 9:21-22, 27; Judges 1:28, 31, 33; 1 Kings 9:20-21). But why curse (by name) Canaan and not Ham? Some believe it is obvious that Ham spoke to Canaan about Noah's nakedness and Canaan went in and dishonored his father (possibly even sexually). Others say it is because the father and son are so much alike that the names are used interchangeably. Because this account is so abbreviated, I don't really have a positive answer.

What Cain was to the antediluvian world, Canaan was to the world after the flood. He was the ancestor of the Canaanites who preceded Israel in the land of Palestine. The preoccupation of that entire Canaanite culture with their vulgar sex gods, which they worshiped with the most abominable rites, indicates clearly that they partook of the nature of their infamous ancestor.

26) *Blessed be the Lord, the God of Shem* – This means, that in a particular sense, God would be identified as "the God of Shem," through whom the Messiah would come for human redemption. This is the prophetic designation of Shem as the patriarch through whom Jesus would be born.

28-29) Since Abraham was born about 292 years after the Flood, it appears that, for 58 years, Noah was a contemporary of Abraham!

One can only grieve at this flaw exhibited in the life of Noah, but the inspired Scriptures detail the sins of its heroes in the same stark truthfulness that recounts their deeds of righteousness and valor.

Genesis – Chapter 10

Nations Descended From Noah

Intro) Christians should not ignore this chapter, the fundamental teaching of which is that all the nations of earth are descended from a single ancestor and that, therefore, all the peoples of the earth are of "one blood" (Acts 17:26).

Read Genesis 10.

2-5) The sons of Japheth.

6-20) The sons of Ham.

21-31) The Sons of Shem

32) This is a summary verse for this chapter.

It is clear enough that these lists are incomplete and selective. The sacred writer did not design them to be exhaustive in this report but merely to show that all the peoples of the earth descended from a single ancestor. This chapter teaches the oneness of all mankind, that we are all the children of the same parents, that we are therefore brothers and sisters each to all, and that we should compel our attitudes and behavior to conform to such a profound truth. Medical science in the current era has added a vital, living proof of the truth of all this, in that there is no distinction whatever among the races as to their types of blood, persons of any race being able to provide the material for a blood transfusion to persons of any other race.

You may study extensively these genealogies if you like. You may also see where they settled and the accuracy of this historical account. Even though these peoples settled in different areas, only the beginning of nations appears here. All of the peoples descended from Noah spread rapidly over the earth, and there were many overlapping districts in which the various families were commingled.

Genesis – Chapter 11

The Tower of Babel

Intro) In this chapter we see the confusion of tongues. The estimated time after the flood is 100 years.

Read Genesis 11:1-9.

1) *Now the whole earth had one language and one speech* – This is easy enough to understand because all people at that time were descendants of Noah, therefore being one family.

2) *They found a plain in the land of Shinar* – A "broad plain." Not a narrow gorge but a great area bordered by mountains. This is the great plain upon which Nimrod built Babylon and other cities.

3) *Make bricks and bake them* – Baked brick is stronger than sun dried brick. Permanence is in their minds.

4) Many have discerned that the construction of the tower of Babel was actually the dethronement of God and establishment of paganism as their system of worship. The traditional account handed down by Josephus says, "It was Nimrod who excited them to such an affront and contempt of God; he was the grandson of Ham, the son of Noah." Josephus also affirmed that Nimrod had taught that it was cowardice to submit to God, and wrong to praise God for benefits, because it was through the courage and daring of men themselves that all blessings and benefits came! Admittedly, such a doctrine as this has been the bible of evil world rulers in all generations.

When reading this verse, it is evident that the children of men who wrought this wickedness in God's sight were clearly infected with the "us" virus – the pride, arrogance, and conceit of the people standing starkly obvious in this account. But what does the text reveal here as the sin?

Lest we be scattered abroad – Violation of 9:1. Their rebellion against God is inherent in their stated purpose of avoiding their being "scattered," a scattering that God had commanded in the original great commission to "multiply and fill the earth."

Note: Matthew 28:18-20; persecution then Acts 8:4-5. How about the church today?

5-7) *And the Lord came down* – Here we have an anthropomorphism – the attribution of human characteristics or behavior to a god, animal, or object. So here we are shown God's interference in this project of evil men. It's interesting to consider, while man was boasting of his tower "to reach heaven," God could not even see it without making a trip down to earth! Despite the fact that God sees everything continually throughout the whole universe, this manner of speech is superlative as an exposure of the foolishness and wickedness of men.

With one language this is only the beginning of the evil they can do. In fact, their rebellion here could lead to the true knowledge of God being totally removed from the earth. Solution: give them different languages! Regarding the wonder of how God confused the languages, we simply have no information whatever. The will of God alone was sufficient to produce the conditions that He desired to appear.

8-9) Separation by languages results in separation into different lands.

"Babel" = "confusion (by mixing)."

Shem's Descendants

Read Genesis 11:10-26.

10-26) The history of Shem. As before, Moses disposes of the history of those less important to his narrative first.

Terah's Descendants

Read Genesis 11:27-32.

27-32) Here we have a history of Terah. The narrative is narrowed to Abram and Lot. Terah leaves Ur and moves to Haran, but Abram will complete the move on into Canaan. This was probably given to explain the association of Lot with Abraham in subsequent chapters of Genesis. He apparently became, in fact, a kind of adopted son of Abraham, following the death of Haran in Ur.

30) This made mention of the barrenness of Sarah.

Note: Abram (Abraham) was in Mesopotamia when he received his call from God to go to Canaan. This is before he went to Haran (Acts 7:1-4).

This brings a great division of Genesis to a close. Whereas, the previous chapters have dealt with universal events, or events concerned with the history of all the Adamic race, the following chapters will take up the narrative relative to the deeds and fortunes of the "Chosen Nation," the posterity of Abraham through whom a Messiah to redeem all men was promised.

Genesis – Chapter 12

Promises to Abram

Intro) Where the first major division of Genesis dealt with the origin and early development of mankind as a whole, the second major division treats the history of the Hebrew patriarchs as it traces the formation of the Israelite people.

The first great Hebrew patriarch, who later became known as the "father of the Hebrew people," was Abraham. Abram's career, as traced in Genesis, is that of a man of faith, and it is this key theme of his life that is given prominence later in the New Testament record. Abram's faith, however, was not an untested or inactive faith, but instead it was an active faith which led him to obey the commands of God. You will notice as we proceed that Abram, much like Noah, had to act on his faith in order to receive his reward.

Read Genesis 12:1-9.

1) *The Lord had said to Abram* – We are not informed as to the manner of God's communicating with Abram here; but Acts 7:2 declares, "The God of glory appeared to our father Abraham." God is Spirit, and it might be conjectured that in this call there occurred one of the great theophanies which, again and again, marked God's dealings with His people.

God gives His instructions to Abram in verse 1. These instructions are to:

1. Go out of his country.
2. Leave his kindred.
3. Depart from his father's house.
4. Go to a land unknown to him, a land that God will show him.

2-3) If he obeys God's instructions, God will in turn keep His covenant with him. The covenant is:

1. Verse 2 – "I will make you a great nation." – The size of this promise is seen against the physical facts prevailing at the time, in that Abraham had no child whatever, and that Sarai his wife was barren!
2. Verse 2 – "I will bless you." – Blessing for Abraham, as for all of God's people, was dependent upon faith proved by obedience.
3. Verse 2 – "I will make your name great."
4. Verse 2 – "You shall be a blessing." – Abraham was chosen and elevated to his high post, not for his own sake, but for the sake of the blessing that he would become to all people.
5. Verse 3 – "I will bless those who bless you and curse those who curse you." –Without any doubt, this great promise today belongs to the spiritual Israel of God in exactly the same manner as it applied under the old covenant to the old Israel. Compare what Jesus says in Luke 18:7.
6. Verse 3 – "In you all the families of the earth shall be blessed." – A promise as big as this one can be fulfilled in only one thing, and that is by the coming of the Son of God to save all people from sin.

4-5) So Abram, having faith and acting on his faith, obeyed. He departed from Haran at age 75 and headed toward Canaan. It was a long journey to Canaan from Haran, being some "four hundred miles to the southwest," as one scholar noted, but Abram with his entire entourage and all of his possessions undertook the journey and made it!

* There are a couple of options regarding this account of the "call" of Abram. In the text here, it appears that the call came to Abram in Haran. But as we already pointed out, Abram was in Ur of the Chaldeans when he received the call. So it appears that either:

1. The call recorded here took place in Ur but the text only gives Abrams age when he leaves Haran.
2. There were two calls. The first took place in Ur and was not written in the text. The second happened in Haran and that's the one we have account of. One thing to consider regarding this possibility is that Abram was commanded to leave his father's house. When you read the account in chapter 11:31-32 it appears Terah, Abram's idol-worshipping father (Joshua 24:2) went along for the journey. This was contrary to the demand given by God, so there was reason for a second call.

6-7) Abram arrived at the land of Shechem. The Canaanites were then populating the land. But though the land was occupied, God says to Abraham that it will be given to him. Abram then built an altar to the Lord.

The Lord, who had appeared to him – These occasions of God's actually appearing to Abraham are understood by many as "pre-incarnate appearances of Christ."

8-9) From Shechem, Abram moved to a place between Bethel and Ai. He then built another altar to the Lord and called on the name of the Lord. Abram then continued toward the south.

Abram in Egypt

Since we have seen that Abram is a man of great faith, a man who trusted God enough to move to an unknown land, it comes as somewhat of a disappointment to learn that Abram can also be a man of great moral weakness. This insight is gathered from an incident which takes place in Egypt, where Abram will take his family because of a famine in Canaan.

Read Genesis 12:10-20.

10-16) In this brief account in Egypt we see a bit of trickery on the part of Abram. Due to a famine in the land, Abram goes from Canaan to Egypt to escape. Afraid for his life and because of the beauty of his wife Sarai, Abram instructs her to pretend she is his sister. As a result of this deceptive act, Sarai is taken in to Pharaoh. Pharaoh treats Abram well for Sarai's sake. Pharaoh loaded Abram with great wealth, intended no doubt as a kind of dowry showing intent to marry her.

13) *You are my sister* – His half-sister (cf. 20:12). This is the literal truth, but not all of the truth. Abram knew that if all the truth was told, Pharaoh would come to a different conclusion about him and Sarai. It is the deceit that makes this a lie.

17-20) Since God had a purpose for Sarai, He overruled the difficulty caused by Abram's deception. God plagues Pharaoh and his house because of Sarai, Abram's wife. By these plagues, God kept Pharaoh from further wrongdoing. Pharaoh rebukes Abram for his deceit and sends him away along with Sarai.

20) This is viewed as a military escort for the protection and safe passage of Abram's company, Pharaoh evidently fearing God's vengeance against him for any harm that might come to Abram.

No effort should be made to gloss over Abram's actions in this matter. The appearance is that he is guilty of two offences:

1. Lack of trust in God's promised protection, that we see inverses2-3.
2. Deception by means of a half-truth.

As I've said before, we learn from such cases that even the great patriarchs were not sinless and that scripture even records the failures of its heroes.

Genesis – Chapter 13

Abram Inherits Canaan

Intro) Abram has dishonored himself in Egypt, but he is not destined to remain in this valley of self-defeat and moral failure. As he and his nephew, Lot, came out of Egypt once again into Canaan, the renewal of Abram's moral character will become evident.

When grazing land becomes scarce and trouble develops between their herdsmen, Abram is put into a position where, as the elder patriarch, he can insist on his right to whatever territory he may choose. But rather than being self-assertive, Abram gives Lot the first choice.

This chapter shows how Abram's separation from Lot finally came about. God, at the first, had commanded Abram to leave "his kindred" and "his father's house," but, somehow, Abraham had never really done this. So it is appropriate to note here that the renewal of the promises to Abraham took place immediately after Lot's departure toward Sodom.

Read Genesis 13.

1) Abram returns with Sarai and Lot, to his tent between Bethel and Ai and once again calls on the name of the Lord.

2) *Abram was very rich in livestock, in silver, and in gold* – This brings into view the vast wealth that Pharaoh had given Abram on account of Sarai.

4-5) *Abram called on the name of the Lord* – Abram worshiped Jehovah.

6-7) There was insufficient pasture and water locally for the extensive herds and flocks. The land that was available to Abram and Lot was limited due to the occupancy of the Canaanites and the Perizzites. So, vying for the limited pasturage and water, the herdsmen came into conflict.

8-13) Because of his character, Abram chooses to keep the important relationship with Lot intact. Abram allows Lot to select his own land and occupy it. Lot, unfortunately, chooses land close to the morally perverted city of Sodom. Choosing on the basis of the fertile fields, Lot moved among some very wicked neighbors.

14-18) After Lot's departure, God again promises to make Abram's descendants as numerous as the dust of the earth and to give them the land of Canaan.

15) *I give to you and your descendants forever* – The word "forever" has several meanings. The context must determine the meaning. As far as the fleshly Israel is concerned, all of God's blessings upon them were contingent, absolutely, upon their acceptance of the rule of God and upon their following in the steps of Abraham's faith, which they resolutely refused to do. They formally rejected God's government in the elevation of Saul to the monarchy, and were ultimately cast off altogether as being God's Chosen People in any racial or secular sense. Every line of the O.T., as well as the N.T., confirms this.

17-18) God tells Abram to get up, see, and walk through this land which God would give to him. Abram would settle in Hebron for some time.

Note: Abram here, by allowing Lot to choose his land, seems to have renewed his faith in God's oversight. This faith seemed to be flawed when they were entering Egypt.

Note: Lot's choice sounds familiar to the intermarriage we discussed earlier which led to the flood. The women were, much like this land, pleasing to the eye, however, corruption was around the corner.

Genesis – Chapter 14

Lot's Captivity and Rescue

Intro) In this chapter we will notice a battle of kings. During this feud, Lot, Abram's nephew, is captured. This text reveals great loyalty and courage in Abram's character. Although the mention of several rulers here gives the chapter an international flavor, scripture is interested in these events because of Lot's involvement, and especially Abram. The Genesis account here begins with a background leading to Lot's dramatic rescue.

Read Genesis 14:1-17.

1-4) Five Canaanite city-states rebel against Chedorlaomer of Elam.

3) *Valley of Siddim (that is, the Salt Sea)* – The meaning here appears to be that the site of the battle mentioned was, at the time of the writing of Genesis, a portion of the Dead Sea.

5-12) Chedorlaomer and his armies defeat the cities of the plain, plunder their cities, and take many of the people (including Lot and his family) as slaves.

10) *The kings of Sodom and Gomorrah fled; some fell there, and the remainder fled to the mountains* – Realizing their defeat, the kings of Sodom and Gomorrah flee.

13) It is important to note that these three allies of Abram contributed armed forces to aid Abram in his rescue (cf. v. 24).

14) Upon learning about Lot's capture, Abram and 318 of his trained servants ride out to rescue Lot.

Trained servants (men) who were born in his own house – It is often overlooked that Abram was the possessor of many indentured servants, and slaves born in his house.

Went in pursuit as far as Dan – This place was in northern Palestine, and it was this fact that brought Abram into the Jerusalem area on his return trip to his residence in Hebron, thus providing the setting for his extremely significant meeting with Melchizedek.

Abram divides his men and initiates a surprise attack at night. Chedorlaomer is defeated and Abram returns with Lot, his goods, and other women and people whom were taken.

Abram and Melchizedek

Read Genesis 14:18-24.

18-20) As Abram returns from battle to his home in Hebron, he meets Melchizedek. The text states that he was "the priest of God Most High." This is Jehovah! He is no pagan priest. A pagan priest would not bless Abram as he does here.

Melchizedek blesses Abram – (Hebrews 7:7) – the greater blesses the lesser.

And he gave him a tithe of all – The "he" in this verse is Abram, indicating that Abram paid the tithes to Melchizedek, a fact of which we are absolutely certain because of Hebrews 7:1-2, which speaks of Melchizedek, "to whom Abraham gave a tenth part of all."

The Mosaic tithe was not in existence yet, however, tithing was already a form of worship.

21-24) In contrast to his response to Melchizedek, Abram refuses to have any fellowship with Bera, king of Sodom. Abram refuses the request of this wicked ruler. Abram refuses the spoils from the king of Sodom but gives the option to his allies. He only lays claim to only what was necessary for sustenance of his men. So here we see that Abram will go to war for what is right, but not for personal gain. How do you think that looked to his household and allies?

Genesis – Chapter 15

God's Covenant with Abram

Intro) With the passing of time, Abram begins to be concerned that he and Sarai still do not have any children. How can his offspring inherit the land if there is no offspring? Abram is surely puzzled and seemingly lacking in faith yet again. So God, once again, reassures Abram that he will have children, who in turn will multiply exceedingly.

There were two elements in the divine promise to Abram:
1. The creation of the first Israel, including the promise of settling them in Canaan and making them a mighty nation, and
2. The bringing in, through them, of the Messiah, through whom redemption and salvation would be made available to all who live on earth.

Read Genesis 15.

1) *The word of the Lord came to Abram in a vision* – We are not told just how this came or just how Abram knew it was not just another dream.

2-3) Abram falsely assumes and fears that upon his death all his goods will be passed on to Eliezer, one of his servants from Damascus. Eliezer will then become the heir to the covenant.
1. All the promises previously made to Abram are dependent upon his having a son.
2. If there is no son, there will be no descendants.
3. Land cannot be given to, nor can all nations be blessed through descendants who do not come into existence.

4-5) God graciously overlooks Abram's insecurity and reassures him of His promise. God tells Abram that the promised heir will be his own son and that Abram's descendants will be as numerous as the stars.

Note that it was not specifically stated here that Sarai would be the mother of the promised heir.

6) Abram believed the Lord.

And He accounted it to him for righteousness – When? This is fulfilled in Genesis 22:9-12, according to James 2:19-24. As always, it is faith and obedience that is acceptable, nothing less!

7-8) Abram asks for a sign of confirmation. Not in doubt, but for assurance.

9-17) God ratifies His promise to Abram with a covenant sealed by blood. At sunset Abram falls into a deep sleep where horror and great darkness fell upon him. God then speaks to Abram in his sleep, telling him that his descendants will be enslaved for four hundred years. God also mentions to Abram that the oppressors will be punished and that his descendants will be set free and depart with great riches. Then a smoking oven and a burning torch passed between the pieces of the dead animals of the sacrifice. This oven and this torch seem to symbolize the presence of God. His passing between the pieces, as was the custom in those days, completed the covenant ceremony with Abram in order that Abram would be assured.

13) They will afflict them four hundred years – The same period is referred to as 430 years in Exodus 12:40, but no contradiction exists. Note that it is not the total stay in Egypt, but the period of their "affliction" which is here prophesied as "four hundred years." They were not afflicted during the early years of their sojourn there while Joseph was yet Pharaoh's deputy. Also, in all probability, the time period here is stated in round numbers, meaning "about four hundred years." The same period is called "four generations" a little later, that being correct in view of the longevity of the patriarchs.

15) Go to your fathers in peace – This cannot apply to the place where Abram was buried, for he was not buried with his fathers, but in the cave of Machpelah. So here it seems is a clear testimony to belief in an eternal life in the patriarchal age.

16) *The iniquity of the Amorites is not yet complete* – When a nation reaches a certain point in wickedness, God will remove it. How about the United States or any country?

Amorites – The largest Canaanite family, therefore it stands for the whole family. When their sins are full, God will have a nation ready to move into the land!

18-21) God reveals to Abram the boundaries of the Promised Land, from the border of Egypt to the Euphrates River.

I have given – Perfect tense. It is as sure as if it had already happened!

This promise is completed! (cf. Nehemiah 9:8; Joshua 21:43-45; 1 Kings 4:21).

Genesis – Chapter 16

Hagar and Ishmael

Intro) About ten years have passed since God renewed His promise that Abram would father children. Although both Abram and Sarai continue to believe that it will happen, Sarai seems to wonder if this promise includes her specifically as the mother of Abram's offspring.

Read Genesis 16.

1-4) Despite her faith in God's promise, Sarai convinces herself that she is not part of God's plan and creates her own to help make the promise come true.

2) *The Lord has restrained me from bearing children* – Sarai is still unable to bear children. Her assessment is accurate. The time has not come yet for the fulfillment. Because of her condition, she convinces Abram to marry Hagar, her servant, in order to have offspring through her. Though this would be personally humiliating, it is altogether proper by the custom of the time for a woman of Sarai's position to give her servant to her husband for the purpose of child bearing. Children born under these circumstances would receive inheritance as if they were natural children. Sarai's suggestion seems to be both unselfish and, at first blush, designed to bring about Abram's promise from God.

However, most scholars find great sin in this account. One of the scholars said the following:

> *"Well, what was wrong with this? It was a legal and commonly accepted practice after the customs of that age, and we can hardly suppose that Abram and Sarai here deliberately chose to violate God's law. However, there are a number of things wrong:*
>
> *1. It violated the concept of monogamous marriage, which had been from the beginning.*
>
> *2. It was a sinful use of a slave girl, who was hardly in a position to deny what was demanded of her, to fulfill the personal desires of Abram and Sarai, and such an inconsiderate use of one's fellow human beings for his own purposes can never be anything but sinful.*
>
> *3. It was a presumption upon their part that God could not fulfill His promise except through their human devices.*
>
> *4. This introduction of polygamy was to continue among the patriarchs of Israel with the most far-reaching and undesirable consequences, as in the example of Jacob. Abram and Sarai could not have exhibited a worse example for the subsequent generations of the Chosen People than that visible here."*

The brother continues:

> *"This is also a convenient place to note that the extensive posterity of Hagar are the proponents of Islam, and thus the nations that came through Hagar not only proved to be inveterate enemies of the Jews, but of the Christians also. Little could Abram and Sarai have known what a Pandora's box of perpetual troubles for all mankind they opened by the little maneuver recorded here."*

After Hagar conceives, she begins to despise her mistress. She is likely proud and feels superior to Sarai, forgetting she is, in fact, her slave. She may even believe that she will replace Sarai in Abram's affections.

5-11) Sarai blames Abram for these conditions and even calls for God to judge between them. As Hagar was Sarai's property, and since the whole situation was due to her initial suggestion, Abram simply turned the problem back to her.

After suffering harsh treatment from the frustrated Sarai, Hagar flees into the desert. Hagar then meets with the Lord. The Angel of the Lord comes to her by a well and questions her as God had questioned Adam in Eden, not for the purpose of procuring information, but with a design of appealing to Hagar's conscience. She was engaged in an illegal flight, which, according to the laws of that age, could have been punished severely, even with death.

The Angel of the Lord then tells her to return to Sarai and to submit to her authority. The Angel of the Lord then tells Hagar that she will have uncountable descendants through her unborn son, whom she shall call Ishmael (God hears).

12) "The antagonistic and war-like disposition of the Arab nations has continued until the present time. Only God could have uttered a prophecy so circumstantially fulfilled over such a long period of time. That race has neither been dissipated by conquest, nor lost by migration, nor confounded with the blood of other countries. They have continued to dwell in the presence of their brethren, a distinct nation, wearing upon the whole the same features and aspects which this prophecy first impressed upon them. And thus it came to pass that the child of Abram and Sarai's unbelief became the progenitor of the Arabs, Israel's bitterest foes throughout history. And from this line also came Muhammad and Islam, one of the most demonic of religions and a foe of Christianity."

15-16) Hagar obeys and Jehovah begins fulfilling His promises to her.

Then finally, when Abram was 86 years old, Hagar bore him a son and he named his son Ishmael.

Special Notes: As we study the book of Genesis, I will show evidences of just who the Angel of the Lord is. In fact, I believe the evidence will show that the Angel of the Lord found here and in other areas of the OT is Christ, the second personality in the Godhead.

* According to John 1:1, the Word (Logos) was God, i.e. divine, the same nature with the Father.

** Since the Word was active in creation, we can hardly suppose that He would drop entirely out of the picture for thousands of years. Or that He would be inactive in the affairs of this world.

*** I believe it is a fact that Jesus was the Angel of the Lord. And I believe that you will see, from the amount of Scripture used, that the position taken is scriptural and not a mere speculation.

The first evidence is found right here in this chapter.

v. 10) *Then the Angel of the Lord said to her, "**I will** multiply your descendants exceedingly –* The angel is speaking as if He were, and is in fact, deity. This is not a created angel but The Angel – Christ! God saying what the Angel said as His own words. But also, Moses has recorded this in the same fashion, by inspiration. Compare Genesis 21:17-18.

v. 13) *Then she called the name of **the Lord who spoke to her**, You-Are-the-God-Who-Sees –* She knew she was speaking to the Lord and, again, we have this record of this written by inspiration through Moses.

Genesis – Chapter 17

The Sign of the Covenant

Intro) The Genesis record is silent as to what events transpire over the next few years. However, the door to history is once again opened some 13 years following Ishmael's birth. At this time God appears once again to Abram to restate His promises and to confirm His prior covenant.

Here begins to appear some of the duties and obligations incumbent upon Israel and deriving from the covenant. Up to this point, it might have seemed that all of the wonderful things that God would do for the posterity of Abraham would be done regardless of any compliance on their part with any of the divine regulations pertaining to the covenant. All such notions were dramatically dispelled in the events of this chapter.

Read Genesis 17.

1) Abram was 99 years old and had gone without the promised son for 24 years since leaving Haran and 13 years since Ishmael's birth.

2) *I will make My covenant* – The covenant is already made (15:18); this means, "to make operative the covenant that is in force." The time has come for the promised son to arrive.

5) Abram receives his new title, Abraham (Father of many). This is the first of two signs to mark this occasion of God's restating His covenant.

6-8) *An everlasting covenant* – The great purpose of this covenant was the delivery of the Messiah to redeem all mankind, and that aspect of it was indeed eternal. However, the land promise was contingent, absolutely, upon Israel's keeping the terms of the covenant and continuing to walk before God and submitting to His government.

Note: All of God's commands are conditional, and failure to obey is forfeiture of every blessing mentioned in connection with the commands.

9-14) After receiving his new title, Abraham receives a new task from God. As the sign of the covenant, he is to circumcise all males in his camp and all baby boys eight days after their birth. Those who refuse to be circumcised are to be cut off from the Israelites.

We need to note that this important command is given in detailed form, much like other commands given to this point, i.e. Noah's detailed instructions for constructing and entering the ark. This detail includes:

1. The extent – every male
2. The operation – circumcised in the flesh of the foreskin
3. The proper age – eight days old
4. The penalty for violation – shall be cut off

You and your descendants after you – Circumcision did not bring them into this covenant relationship but was the sign of it. They were born into the covenant relationship, and by circumcision they were made aware of their obligations under it. This did not mean individual salvation; that still required faith and obedience.

15) God then moves His attention to Sarai, giving her a new title as well. God changes her name from Sarai (princess) to Sarah (noblewoman). As He promises descendants in His restatement, God emphasizes the promise by symbolically changing the names of the chosen pair.

16) God then reassures Abraham that he will be with Sarai as well. God promises that this barren woman will indeed become the mother of nations. This is the first time (that we have record of) that Abraham has been specifically informed that Sarah is to be mother of the child of promise.

17) *Abraham ... laughed* – In doubt? God does not treat it as such.

Fell on his face – This language is used in the text as an act of worship. This is laughter of joy and surprise. Abraham is obviously amazed that, after all these years, and despite the increasing human odds against it, he and Sarah will actually have a child of their own—just as promised.

18-21) Although Abraham is overjoyed at the prospect of fathering a son through Sarah, it is obvious that Abraham has become attached to his son Ishmael. Abraham asks that Ishmael be able to share in God's blessings. God assures Abraham that Ishmael will have many descendants and will be the ancestor of twelve princes and a great nation. God, however, makes it clear that it will be through Isaac's lineage that the covenant will be honored.

23-27) As the second sign of the occasion, God institutes the rite of circumcision as detailed earlier. Abraham, without hesitation, obeys the divine command. Faith leads to obedience.

Although he was not the child of promise, Ishmael, like other males of Abraham's household, is included among the recipients of covenant blessings. The writer concludes, in verse 27, by showing the obedience of Abraham in full detail, just as the commandment had been given in full detail earlier.

Genesis – Chapter 18

The Son of Promise

Intro) Not long after Abraham has responded to God's instructions regarding circumcision, God once again appears to Abraham.

Read Genesis 18:1-15.

1-2) The Lord appears to Abraham by the terebinth trees of Mamre. Abraham looked up, saw the three men and ran to meet them. The "three men" were not men at all, but the Lord Himself accompanied by two angels. Nevertheless, they had every appearance of being men, even eating dinner with Abraham.

3) Abraham uses the term "my Lord" upon greeting the visitors. It is possible that, since the Hebrew word used can mean "Lord God," that Abraham knew at the beginning that God was among the visitors. However, it should be noted that the word translated "Lord" here is NOT the same word as that in vv. 1, 13, 14, 17, 19, 20 and 22 which is designated for Jehovah. Nor is it the same word translated Lord in vv. 27, 30, 31 and 32 where Abraham is calling Him Lord in their conversation. This word is more emphatic. He is using the term here to speak to whom he called "The judge of all the earth."

Since the word can also be used to mean "master," "father," and other similar meanings, it is also possible that this address was simply one of courtesy which Abraham may have been addressing to the apparent leader of the group. If this is the case, Abraham may not have been aware that God was in his presence at this time. Hebrews 13:2 is apparently a reference to this very event; and there it is stated that the host entertained "angels unaware." If that is the case, we may interpret Abraham's bowing himself to the earth not as an act of worship, but as a warm friendly greeting only, after the manner and customs of the times. Note that he considered them to be in need of "strengthening," etc., which he could hardly have done had he known their real identity. Scholars differ on this and I can't tell you for certain either way, but the evidence does seem to lean toward the fact that Abraham learned later the nature of these "men."

6-8) Abraham then prepares a meal for his visitors, complete with fine meal made into cakes, a tender and good calf freshly prepared, butter, and milk.

10-12) *Sarah your wife shall have a son* – It had been only a short while since this name had been given to Sarah, yet "He" knew it; also. "He" knew of their desire for a son, and apparently also, that God had promised that Sarah would be the mother. So, with this interchange, Sarah, and certainly Abraham, possibly began to know the supernatural nature of their guests.

Sarah, who was listening in her tent, overheard the Lord. Sarah then, because of her advanced age, and the stage of her life, laughs in her heart. This seems to be a laugh of disbelief, but it also may possess a bit of hopeful anticipation as well. Nevertheless, we cannot fault Sarah as being faithless, for the writer of Hebrews declared that, "By faith Sarah herself also received strength to conceive seed, and she bore a child when she was past the age, because she judged Him faithful who had promised" (Hebrews 11:11). Whatever Sarah's initial impression might have been, she was promptly to receive concrete and convincing evidence that God Himself was their guest.

13-14) The Lord acknowledges Sarah's laugh. This may have been the point that Abraham realized that he had a divine being among him; however, as we mentioned before, he may have already been aware.

The Lord then declares to Abraham and Sarah that nothing is too hard for the Lord. Sarah will have a son.

15) When God questions Sarah's laugh, she impulsively denies any expression of doubt. But when God insists that she is not telling the truth, it can be visualized that Sarah stood silent and fearful in recognition that this visitor had correctly perceived her disbelief.

Abraham Intercedes For Sodom

Intro) God may be perturbed by Sarah's impulsive deception that we discussed earlier, however, it is nothing compared with the righteous wrath He is soon going to display against the wicked cities of Sodom and Gomorrah in the Jordon Plain, presumably near what is today known as the Dead Sea (Coincidence?).

It is in Sodom that Abraham's nephew, Lot, lives with his wife and two daughters. With this in mind, it is understandable that, when God tells Abraham He is going to destroy Sodom, Abraham would plead that at least the righteous in Sodom be saved. But Abraham's humble, yet bold, intercession with God extends to even those outside of Lot's family, should they be righteous. God's response to Abraham's calculated bargaining reveals God's sublime righteousness and mercy.

Read Genesis 18:16-33.

17-19) *Shall I hide from Abraham what I am doing* – God determined to tell Abraham about His plan for the city of Sodom; but why?

1. Abraham is a friend of God.
2. Abraham has been chosen to be the father of a righteous people.
3. It seems the Lord choses to inform Abraham of the coming destruction because the example of punishment for disobedience will serve as a warning to Abraham's descendants as they strive to "keep the way of the Lord" (After all, is that not why we have the record today and teach about it to our kids, families, and the lost?).
4. 4. *For I have known him, in order that he may command his children and his household after him.* – The literal translation of this is, "For I know him, that he will command his children and his household after him."

20-21) God tells Abraham about the wickedness of Sodom. The outcry of the innocent victims of Sodom and Gomorrah's wickedness has been heard. God, being the righteous judge that He is, goes down to investigate the severity of the behavior. Here again we see the use of anthropomorphism. Of course, God's omniscience enables Him to know all things instantly; but this language accommodates itself to the behavior and customs of men.

22-33) Note that the two angels are sent on their way to Sodom, but the Lord himself remained and heeded the plea of Abraham. Abraham boldly challenges God on behalf of the righteous residents of the wicked city.

- Abraham asks, "Will You destroy the righteous with the wicked?" Abraham intercedes on behalf of Lot and others that are righteous by asking this great question.
- Abraham argues, "Far be it from You to do such a thing." It would not cooperate with God's righteousness to destroy the righteous with the wicked.
- Abraham then urges, "Shall not the judge of all the earth do right?" Abraham grounds his plea in the character of God. God is not an arbitrary and unreasonable deity, but is instead a God of justice and righteousness.
- Because of God's righteousness, righteous people exert a preservative influence in society (we have already witnessed this influence once with Noah and his family).

Abraham begins by pleading for 50 righteous souls. By the end of the meeting, because of Abraham's persistence and God's previously mentioned character, the number of righteous souls necessary to halt destruction has been reduced to a mere 10.

One deduction that must be made from this passage is that Sodom did not have ten righteous people in it; for God judged them and destroyed the city the very night following this intercession. The next chapter will begin with the experience of the two angels who had proceeded on to Sodom with a view to spending the night there.

Note: It is important to realize that, even though Abraham was bold enough to challenge God on behalf of these righteous, he never forgot that he was lowly in contrast to God's greatness.

* Earlier in our study we introduced the idea that Christ is mentioned as active here in the OT. That seems to be the case here too. Abraham stood before the Lord (Jehovah) and talked with him (18:1). Three men appeared before Abraham (18:2). The men went on but the Lord (Jehovah) remained (18:22). Only two of the three men reached Sodom (19:1). The one to whom Abraham talked is called Lord (Jehovah) (18:13, 17, 20, 22).

Genesis – Chapter 19

Sodom's Depravity

Intro) In the light of the N.T., this chapter appears as one of very great significance, because the destruction of Sodom was specifically mentioned by the Savior himself as a type of the Second Coming of Christ and the destruction of the whole world at the end of the age. Read Luke 17:28-32.

The apostle Peter shed further light on this chapter by pointing out that just as God delivered righteous Lot, so the righteous would be delivered out of temptation. God does not destroy the righteous with the wicked. Read 2 Peter 2:6-10.

The sacred writer, Jude, made the destruction of Sodom to be a type of "the eternal fire" that shall consume the wicked at the time of the Judgment. Read Jude 7

Read Genesis 19:1-11.

1-3) The two angels arrive in Sodom. Lot sees them, greets them and insists that they spend the night in his home. Lot is most likely well aware of the type of people in Sodom and the consequent danger of their camping in the street, which was what the visitors had suggested in verse 2. We can see righteousness and hospitality in the character of Lot.

4-5) After a feast, before the visitors could lay down to sleep, the men of Sodom, both young and old, surrounded the house and demanded that Lot hand over the guests. Notice the wickedness of the whole city! (V. 4):

- Old,
- Young,
- All the people,
- From every quarter and
- They surrounded the house.

5) *That we may know them carnally* – The verb "know" used here means "to have sexual relations with," so the men of Sodom were hoping to have homosexual relations with the new men in town. Because of this account, and the wickedness of the city, it is understandable that such unnatural relations are now termed "Sodomy."

6-8) Lot offered his virgin daughters to the men instead of the guests. This was a bad substitute and could have led to an even greater sin.

9-11) The men, after denying Lot's counter-offer, pressed hard against him. The angels reached out and rescued Lot whom was trying desperately to rescue them. The men of Sodom were then stricken with blindness. Lot probably began to realize the nature of these angels when they smote the would-be intruders with blindness.

Sodom and Gomorrah Destroyed

Read Genesis 19:12-29.

12-14) The angels told Lot to inform his entire family of the coming destruction. He warns his sons-in-law, however, they believed nothing more than that he was joking.

Sometimes it seems as if we are considered "mad," "off our rockers," or as joking when we warn our relatives and those around us about the judgment awaiting the unconverted.

15-17) In the morning the angels urged Lot by saying, "Arise, take your wife and your two daughters who are here, lest you be consumed in the punishment of the city." What a tragic situation! Sons and married daughters, their extensive possessions, all that they had, remained in the doomed city, and it was almost impossible for Lot to tear himself away from it all—and his poor wife failed utterly to do so. Not even Lot would have been spared, but the special mercy of God exceeded all that could have been imagined in order to save him anyway. The angels grabbed him and brought him out.

The Angels told Lot and his family to:
- Escape
- Not look behind them
- Not stay in the plain
- Escape to the mountains
- If they did not obey, they would die.

18-22) Lot pleads to stay in Zoar. The men agreed.

23-26) The wrath of God falls upon Sodom and the other wicked cities of the plain. There were a total of five cities in the plain. Cf. 14:8.

1. Sodom – Destroyed – Deuteronomy 29:23
2. Gomorrah – Destroyed – Deuteronomy 29:23
3. Admah – Destroyed – Deuteronomy 29:23
4. Zeboim – Destroyed – Deuteronomy 29:23 – Used as an example – Hos. 11:8
5. Zoar – Spared – Genesis 19:21-22 – Used as an example – Hos. 11:8

The Lord rained fire and brimstone on Sodom and Gomorrah. He devastated these cities, all the cities in the plain, all the inhabitants of the city, and whatever grew on the ground.

Lot's wife, who was apparently convinced but not converted, "looked back," and is, because she did not heed the previous warning, destroyed. Jesus said, "Remember Lot's wife." Do not hesitate! Hold fast to God's way of escape:

   a. She is a warning to all who are tempted to sacrifice their safety in order to win or keep more of this world's goods.
   b. If we strive to possess the best of both worlds, we are likely to lose both.
   c. She is a reminder that being "near safety" is not enough.

    d. She is a warning that having begun to follow the Lord's Word, one may still turn back from the way and be lost.

27-29) From the place where he stood pleading boldly before the Lord, Abraham viewed the devastated land. God did, in fact, remember that pleading and spared Lot's life along with his wife and two daughters. God heard the prayer of a righteous man (James 5:16). Lot himself was counted righteous (2 Peter 2:6-7).

The Descendants of Lot

Intro) As Abraham looks out from the heights of Hebron over the now-desolate Jordan Plain, no doubt with amazement and obvious concern for Lot, he has no way of knowing whether Lot was sufficiently righteous to be saved. There is no record that Abraham ever sees Lot again or even learns of his escape.

What follows is the last historical record of Lot. Strangely, it involves a somewhat bizarre scheme on the part of his two daughters to bear children by their father.

Read Genesis 19:30-38.

30-35) Lot's daughters are afraid they may not marry or bear children. They may have thought that because of their current isolation no man would find them. The daughters "seem" to have a good motive, but, in order to accomplish their goal they get Lot drunk and sleep with him in order to become pregnant. These sisters apparently knew their father would not consent to incest. Considering they lived in Sodom, it is not surprising that they came up with such a scheme.

Some say that Lot was unwilling and was an unwitting tool of his daughters, but, it is all made possible by his apparent willingness to let his daughters get him drunk. You can decide the significance of his role for yourself.

36-38) Moab, father of the Moabites, is born to Lot's older daughter. Ben-Ammi, father of the Ammonites, is born to Lot's younger daughter.

*The fact of Sodom's destruction having been made a type of the final Judgment would appear to suggest that the proliferation and acceptance of the sins of Sodom will again reach a climax before the coming of that great and dreadful Day. God help men to heed the warning!

Genesis – Chapter 20

Abraham and Abimelech

Intro) The human condition is always surprising. It has been 20 years since Abraham was in Egypt and lied to the Pharaoh about Sarah's being his sister and not his wife. In the intervening two decades Abraham has been reassured repeatedly that God will continue to bless him and keep His promises. Abraham has been honored with the very presence of God and made to witness the destructive power of God's judgment against Sodom and Gomorrah. Yet, almost unbelievably, the Genesis account records that Abraham once again lies about his true relationship with Sarah. This time it is to a king by the name of Abimelech.

Read Genesis 20.

1-2) The lie of chapter 12 is repeated. Just as in Egypt, in Gerar Abraham practices deception through means of a half-truth. Again scripture shows itself willing to record and reveal, quite frankly, the errors of its great heroes. There continues to be doubt cast upon the character of this great man of faith. Despite all of his outstanding qualities, Abraham appears to have a tendency toward deception.

Abimelech is not a personal name. Similar to Pharaoh, it is the name of the king.

3-7) God informs Abimelech in a dream that Sarah is married. That such a thing as this occurred was made possible by Abimelech's believing in God, which did not seem to be the case in the incident involving Pharaoh. The king claims, and God acknowledges, that Abimelech was an innocent participant. Therefore He once again steps in to stop the innocent party from committing great sin. God instructs Abimelech to return Sarah to Abraham and promises that he will receive prayer from Abraham.

8-13) Abraham is reproved again for his actions. Abimelech asked Abraham the question, "What have you done to us? How have I offended you that you have brought on me and on my kingdom a great sin?" Abraham tells Abimelech that he was afraid that there was no fear of God and, therefore, a lack of basic morality in the land of Gerar. He was sure that he would be killed for Sarah.

Abraham then suggests that he had not actually told a falsehood, since Sarah was indeed his half-sister. Still it was a lie, spoken with intent to deceive. This is where we learn of their relationship.

13) It appears as if this were a habit of long standing, practiced over and over again throughout many years, and the indication in this is that Abraham was merely pleading that, "I, or we, always do this when we are traveling in strange territory."

14-18) Abimelech restores Sarah to Abraham. Abimelech also compensates Abraham for his trouble with sheep, oxen, silver, and servants. He then rebukes Sarah. Abraham obeys God, prays for Abimelech and the curse is lifted from his household.

Genesis – Chapter 21

Isaac Is Born

Intro) It cannot be long after the experience with Abimelech that Sarah conceives a child by Abraham. With Abraham at 100 and Sarah at 90 years of age, childbirth would seem impossible in human terms. Sarah is clearly astonished, for she and Abraham have waited 25 years for this promised son. Sometimes they believed fully and sometimes they were full of doubt and outright disbelief.

Read Genesis 21:1-7.

1-7) Verses 1-2 stress the fact that God keeps and fulfills His promises. Finally, we see the arrival of the long-sought child of promise. For 25 years Abraham and Sarah have waited for the birth of this son, upon whose coming hinged all of God's promises to Abraham. Again, there could be no great nation without a son; no land could be given to a nation that did not exist; and no blessing could flow from a nation that did not exist. So we see, removing the obstacles of her barrenness, Sarah bore a son.

The name Isaac, meaning "laughter," must have recalled to the proud parents Abraham's laughter of surprise back in chapter 17 and Sarah's laugh in chapter 18, as well as the joy expressed here in verse 6.

We can see great rejoicing is breathed in this entire passage as the aged patriarch and his faithful wife realize their hope and God's promises in the birth of this son.

Hagar and Ishmael Depart

Intro) Probably three years have passed since Isaac was born, and it is the time of Isaac's weaning. The customary feast at the time of a child's weaning is normally an occasion of celebration. But the feast for Isaac becomes an occasion for resentment. Sarah knows that Ishmael, now 17, is mocking young Isaac, and that he also represents a threat to Isaac's right of inheritance. It is therefore Sarah's wish that Abraham cast out Ishmael, along with his mother, Hagar.

Naturally Abraham is reluctant to do this, not only because of his natural ties to Ishmael, but also because of the customary law of his day which forbids the expulsion of a slave wife and her children. But God, for his own reasons, instructs Abraham to do as Sarah has requested, and Abraham makes the painful separation.

Read Genesis 21:8-21.

8-10) The purpose of Abraham's feast, as we mentioned earlier, is to celebrate Isaac's weaning. Sarah sees Ishmael scoffing at Isaac. Sarah is also afraid that Abraham may give Ishmael equal inheritance with Isaac. Sarah requested that Abraham cast out Hagar and Ishmael from the camp.

11-13) Abraham and Sarah are now reaping the bitterness created by themselves when they chose to introduce a slave girl into Abraham's bedchamber as his wife. How far better it would have been if they had found the faith and strength to await the fulfillment of God's promise in His own good time! Abraham, though distressed about Sarah's request, is reassured by God that Hagar and Ishmael will be provided for.

14-16) Abraham then sends them off with a supply of food and water. It should not be supposed that this was the total endowment given to Hagar and her son when Abraham sent them away. It would be totally out of character for Abraham to have sent them away without sufficient provisions, or monies with which to procure them, sufficient for the journey she was compelled to make. The love of Abraham for Ishmael would have prevented such an injustice. This whole narrative is extremely abbreviated. The water supply did not give out because it was small, but because she had been lost and had "wandered" in the wilderness (Genesis 21:14).

In the wilderness Hagar fears she and Ishmael will die. They have wandered and used up their water supply. They both likely become exhausted. After probably trying to support her son, Hagar put Ishmael under one of the desert shrubs, which might provide at least some shade for the hours that she was sure would be his last.

17-18) The meaning of Ishmael's name, "God hears," is once again realized here in vs. 17. God heard the voice of Ishmael. God then tells Hagar to not worry, and reminds her of His promise to make Ishmael a great nation.

19-21) By God's guidance, Hagar was directed to one of the wells of the area, and consequently received much-needed water. Once settled, Hagar took a wife for Ishmael from Egypt. This was normally the role played by the father, but without that figure, Hagar bore the responsibility.

So God delivers Ishmael from sure death and develops him so that he may become a father himself.

A Covenant with Abimelech

Intro) In the time which has passed since Abraham came into the land ruled by Abimelech, Abraham has greatly prospered, not only in having a son born in his old age, but also in the increase of his flocks and herds. It is only natural, then, that Abimelech should become concerned about Abraham's growing power. The Genesis account records Abimelech's diplomatic move to protect his own political position by entering into a treaty of mutual peace with Abraham.

Read Genesis 21:22-34.

22-24) Abimelech does recognize that Abraham is blessed by deity, and therefore desires a covenant of peace with him. Abraham promptly took the requested oath, remembering, no doubt, that Abimelech had indeed granted manifold favors to him, including the rich gifts upon the occasion of his intended marriage to Sarah.

25-26) Abraham seized upon the occasion to resolve a conflict over possession of a well which had been claimed by some of Abimelech's servants. Abimelech disclaims knowledge of the wrong and implies willingness to check into the matter of Abraham's claims. I don't know if he was truthful in his claim of ignorance. Maybe this visit was the result of the incident mentioned here. This conflict between Abraham's servants and Abimelech's people may have caused Abimelech to act to secure his friendly relationship with the powerful Abraham. But, maybe it's all just coincidence. We don't really know his motivation. What we do know is that a water well on the edge of the desert was the power of life and death in the hands of the persons controlling it.

27) Abraham and Abimelech enter into a mutual agreement that neither party would harm the other. The covenant was established, most likely, following the procedures previously mentioned in the record of God's covenant with Abraham.

28-31) The ewe lambs were a separate group of animals designated to Abimelech as a gift. By receiving this gift, Abimelech will recognize that the well in question is Abraham's.

32-34) In order to memorialize the covenant between himself and Abimelech, Abraham planted a tamarisk tree and called on the name of the Lord.

God's great mercy and blessing were poured out upon Ishmael and his posterity, despite the fact of their not being members of the covenant. Nevertheless, God loved them, as indeed he loved the whole world, "So that he gave his only begotten Son."

A Homily by F. Hastings:

God cares for those outside the pale of the Church, even as for those within. Those without have not taken up their privileges, nor do they see how Christ loves them. They are suffering great loss, and are in danger of even greater losses; but God loves them, cares for them, and pities them. 'He is not willing that any should perish, but that all should come to repentance.'

God pitied the people of Nineveh and sent them a warning; he healed Naaman; he sent Elijah to dwell with the woman of Zarephath, thus honoring her; he brought Nebuchadnezzar to his right mind by a judicial affliction; Jesus praised the Syrophoenician woman, and the centurions of the Roman garrison in Capernaum – all these things were loving mercies poured out beyond the boundaries of the Covenant! Oh, how much more widely flows the channel of Divine love and mercy than many are inclined to think!

Whoever, whatever, wherever any man is, let him remember that God loves him."

Genesis – Chapter 22

Abraham's Faith Confirmed

Intro) Even as Ishmael has grown into manhood, his younger half-brother, Isaac, has also developed into a healthy young lad who is surely a good source of joy for Abraham and Sarah. But like many men and women of great faith who must face difficult trials, Abraham is about to face the severest test of all – and it will be Isaac's life which is on the line.

Read Genesis 22:1-19.

1-2) *God tested Abraham* – The versions that render the word "tempt" instead of "test" or "prove" are misleading, because God does not TEMPT any man (James 1:13).

God commands Abraham to offer Isaac as a burnt offering in the land of Moriah. Think of the impact of these designations of Isaac: Your son, your only son Isaac, whom you love. These words from God must have surely startled Abraham. Not only did he love Isaac deeply with all the affection of a father, but Isaac was also the key figure in the promises that God had made to him. Furthermore, human sacrifice, though practiced by some of the ancient Near East peoples, most certainly collided with the goodness of God that was revealed to Abraham.

God here is asking for Abraham's spiritual surrender. God gave this great son, Isaac, to Abraham. Now the suggestion is to give him back.

It is interesting here to note "this is the first mention of love in the O.T." Oddly enough, the first mention of love in the N.T. ("This is my beloved Son ..." Matthew 3:17) refers to Christ, of whom Isaac was a type.

3) Abraham, evidently believing that God would raise Isaac from the dead, if necessary, in order to fulfill His promise, obeys and takes Isaac and two servants on this journey. He rose early to do God's will.

4-5) On the third day, Abraham orders his servants to stay behind with the donkey while he and his son continued to the specific point. There are a couple things worth noting here.

1. Abraham calls this worship.
2. Notice he said, "Stay here…WE will come back to you." Compare this with Hebrews 11:17-19.

6-8) Isaac asks, "Father…where is the lamb for the burnt offering?" How this question from the innocent young boy must have pained Abraham. Abraham evades the question compassionately by stating, "God will provide for Himself the lamb for the burnt offering." Abraham did not realize at this point how true this statement really was. The thoughts that surely passed through the minds of Abraham and Isaac during their fateful journey have been left to the imagination of the reader.

9) Isaac allows his father, Abraham, to bind him on the altar. Again, we are left to imagine the thoughts running through the minds of these two.

10-12) As Abraham prepares for the fatal blow, God stops Abraham from killing his son. The Angel of the Lord acknowledges that the test of faith has been met by Abraham's obedience.

13-14) Instead of offering his son, Abraham offered a ram that he noticed was caught in the thicket.

15-19) *Because you have done this thing, and have not withheld your son, your only son* – How could God say that, when Abraham was also the father of Ishmael? The meaning, of course, is that Isaac was the son of promise, the only legitimate son born to his lawful wife.

Because of Abraham's willingness to sacrifice his only son to God, God in turn promises, once again, that his descendants will be as numerous as the stars of the sky and the sand on the seashore.

Here, again, we have the Angel of the Lord who spoke to Abraham from heaven, who called Himself Lord and made promises only God can make. Here is the renewal of the same promise made by Jehovah. Compare Genesis 12:1-3. Who is this Angel (this Messenger) of the Lord?

Why did God command such a thing? There are many opinions. But, I think one stands out among the others. It is the following: Not until Abraham acted upon his faith did that faith come to fruition. Verse 1 states that "God tested Abraham." Until he lifted the knife over his son, his ultimate surrender to God had not occurred. Faith is not just a nice attitude toward God; it is submission to His will. To will it in the heart is not enough. The act is the ultimate test. This view appears certain in the light of James' statement that Abraham was justified "when he offered up Isaac" (James 2:21).

Notice the faith of Isaac in God and his father!

In this text, we see a type of the Lord Jesus Christ in the person of Isaac.

- The birth of Isaac was supernatural, as was Christ's.
- Both were sons of "promise."
- Both were called "the only begotten son."
- Both carried the "wood" up Calvary (assuming this is the location of the events in Genesis 22).
- Both Isaac and Jesus consented to suffer death.
- Both consented to be "bound."
- Both were laid "upon the wood."
- Both were "offered" by their fathers.
- Both "sacrifices" occurred on the same hill (assuming this is the location of the events in Genesis 22).
- Both were in the prime and vigor of life.

- Both were about age 33 (Some have suggested Isaac was at this age in Genesis 22).
- Both were "dead" three days and nights, Christ literally, Isaac in a figure.
- Both lived again after the "offering," Christ literally, Isaac "in a figure."

The Family of Nahor

Intro) Sometime after Abraham's return to Beersheba from his brief trip with Isaac to the land of Moriah, Abraham receives word regarding his brother Nahor, whom Abraham has not seen since he left Ur of the Chaldeans some 40 years ago. The good news is that Nahor now has eight children by his wife and four by his concubine.

Read Genesis 22:20-24.

20-24) The historical significance of this record of Nahor's family is found in his youngest son, Bethuel, and more importantly Bethuel's daughter, Rebekah, who will soon become an important figure in Abraham's own lineage.

Genesis – Chapter 23

Sarah's Death and Burial

Intro) The years have passed and Abraham is now 137 years old. Isaac, a century behind his father, is a relatively young 37. Sarah, who has the distinction of being the only woman in all of scripture whose age is mentioned, has reached 127. The Genesis account now abruptly records Sarah's death, in the region of Hebron in the land of Canaan, to which Abraham has returned sometime during the last 40 years.

Read Genesis 23.

1-2) Sarah dies at Hebron at 127 years of age. The death of Sarah is the only event of a woman's death and burial to be recorded in the Bible thus far, indicating the importance of Sarah. Peter pointed Christian women to the example of Sarah in 1 Peter 3:6. And the author of Hebrews extolled her faith along with that of the greatest of the patriarchs in Hebrews 11:11.

Scripture pauses to take note of Abraham's mourning over the loss of his beloved companion. This is a touching memorial to this great woman of faith who would become the mother of a great nation.

3-4) Abraham describes himself as a foreigner and a visitor in Canaan, therefore, he has no place to bury Sarah. Prior to this time Abraham owned no land in Canaan. Although the land was promised to his descendants, Abraham merely rented or obtained in other ways the use of land belonging to others. He is simply a "resident alien."

6) *You are a mighty prince among us* – The NKJV missed the mark a little here. The literal translation of this is, "You are a prince of the supreme God." The righteous nobility of Abraham shines in such a compliment. The heathen populations knew that he was God's man. And moved with sympathy for him, they offered him their burying-places.

9) Abraham's suggestion to "give me property" in verse 4 was simply a request to allow him to purchase the land. You can see that here when Abraham offers to pay the "full price." Abraham was talking about a legal transaction to be concluded in the city gate, after the usual custom, and in the presence of witnesses.

10-11) Abraham asks for the cave at the end of Ephron's field. Ephron offers the field too. This was most likely a courteous formality which was normal for transactions of that area.

14-20) Ephron's price was 400 shekels of silver (about 10 pounds). Abraham agreed and took ownership of the field and the cave in order to lie to rest Sarah his wife. Her death and burial in Canaan tied the posterity of Abraham irrevocably to the land of promise. What faith Abraham had in God's promises to go through with this!

Genesis – Chapter 24

A Bride For Isaac

Intro) The death of Sarah seems to have caused Abraham to reflect on the few remaining years in his own life, and to be concerned about preserving his lineage. So Abraham makes preparation for Isaac to marry a woman from among his own kinsmen back in the Mesopotamian Region, from which he had emigrated some 60 years earlier.

Read Genesis 24.

1-4) Abraham instructs his servant to find a wife for Isaac from Abraham's native land of Mesopotamia. It was to be a man from his brethren (not from the Canaanites). It seems Abraham is fearful that if Isaac marries a woman from among the local Canaanites he might be drawn into the worship of their pagan gods.

Some scholars believe this servant to be Eliezer of chapter 15 vs. 2. However, others believe it to be nearly impossible that he could be healthy enough to carry out a mission such as this.

The hand under the thigh accompanied, and in some way symbolized, the making of a solemn pledge as the following text shows.

5-10) The servant suggests taking Isaac back to the land of Mesopotamia if no woman is willing to come back with him. Abraham, recalling the promise made by God that they will be given the land that they are in, will not allow Isaac to go back. Abraham tells the servant that God will intervene and send His angel before him to the land. Abraham further commits that, if with God's intervention, the woman is still not willing to follow him, he will be released from the oath. The servant then swears an oath to Abraham that he will do exactly as Abraham has instructed, loads ten camels with gifts and departs toward Mesopotamia.

11-23) Being informed previously that God would aid him, the servant arrived at a well outside of the city, where the women drew water. He then prayed to God. He then asked the Lord to cause the chosen woman to volunteer to provide water for him and his camels.

That God Himself guided the servant here is undeniable. The test which he devised, and regarding which he prayed to God, was extremely appropriate, because it was related fundamentally to the character, attitude, and personality of the woman to be chosen.

Before the servant finished his prayer, Rebekah appears at the well and fulfills the sign that the servant is seeking. Then, after giving her some gold jewelry, the servant asked who her father was and if he could lodge with them. This was to determine whether or not she belonged to Abraham's kindred.

24-28) Once the servant had realized that he had been successfully aided by God, he bowed down and worshipped God, thanking Him for His mercy and truth toward his master Abraham.

24) *I am the daughter of Bethuel* – It seems that the father (Bethuel) is dead. It appears that she has a brother by the name Bethuel. As we read through the text, this may come to light a little more.

29-53) Rebekah tells her brother (Laban) of these events and Laban invites him in. Food is prepared for the man. The servant would not sit down to eat until he had made known his mission and the significance of it. This whole long paragraph is a recapitulation of the events and conversations, including even the prayer, verbatim, of all that was previously related in the chapter. He clearly understood that Jehovah's hand was in all that had taken place. The servant gives Rebekah more jewelry and invites her to accompany him back to Canaan to marry Isaac.

49) *That I may turn to the right hand or to the left* – To find a wife elsewhere or determine how to proceed with Laban and Bethuel.

50) *We cannot speak to you either bad or good* – They see the providence of God and cannot add to or take away from what has been shown to them. Notice both Laban and Bethuel respond. However, in this account, we do not see the customary authority of the father of the household. It appears that Laban is in charge or shares authority with the Bethuel mentioned here.

54-61) Rebekah, and her family, agree to the terms. After being blessed by her family, Rebekah arose with her maids and followed Abraham's servant.

59) *So they sent away Rebekah their sister* – The only other person in view, besides Laban, in this chapter who could also have been Rebekah's brother was Bethuel, giving inferential support to the understanding that Bethuel mentioned here was not her father, who was dead, but her brother.

59) The nurse mentioned was named Deborah (35:8).

62-67) As the servant and the bride-to-be return, they are noticed by Isaac who is walking through a field. Rebekah dismounts her camel and covers herself when she realizes he is the man she will marry. Isaac takes Rebekah in and she becomes his wife. They marry and provide each other with love and comfort. This comfort was certainly welcome after the loss of Isaac's mother.

* Let's take a moment to note the sacrifices that Rebekah made:
- She did not plead for time to make up her mind.
- She would say goodbye to her home and relatives, with the near certainty that she would never see them again.
- She believed the messenger completely, an incredible act of faith.
- She made the decision, saying, "I will go."
- She followed the messenger to meet her bridegroom.
- She was already the bride-elect, but her actual union with Isaac would not occur until many days had passed, and that final "evening" arrived.
- Then, in the twilight, with her veil upon her, she went forth to meet the bridegroom!

So it is with the bride of Christ

Many of the bride's "relatives" are endowed and enriched because of the Church of Christ. Even worldly and sinful communities are blessed by the presence and activity of Christians. Countless church-related institutions are supported effectively because of their connection with Christianity.

Christians, who are, in fact, "The Bride of Christ," must say "goodbye" to home, to loved ones, to all they had previously loved in order to follow Christ. They must, like Rebekah, believe the testimony of the "Messenger," which is the Holy Spirit, specifically, the Bible, which is the testimony of the "Messenger." They must make the courageous decision, without hesitation or delay. To procrastinate is to lose everything. Like Rebekah, they do not find themselves united finally with Christ until many days have passed, and at last there arrives that final "evening" when they pass through the veil to be with the Lord. Also, they must never leave off following the "Messenger." By such means alone shall they achieve the union with the Bridegroom.

Genesis – Chapter 25

Abraham and Keturah

Read Genesis 25:1-6.

1-4) One of the closing details in the record of Abraham is this brief account of his marriage to Keturah. Keturah had only reached the status of concubine. She bears Abraham six sons including Midian. The Midianites were the most famous of Abraham's descendants by Keturah. They were scattered widely in Arabia and Sinai. They are mentioned in several later biblical episodes.

Keturah was part of God's fulfillment of the promise to make Abraham the "father of many nations" (17:4).

5-6) Isaac clearly enjoys superior status as the child of promise; he is Abraham's only full heir. Abraham, by giving gifts and sending away his descendants by "the concubines," really settles his estate while he is still living. He does this in order that all should understand Isaac's status, and so that there would be no dispute. That is also why the text states that he gave all that he had to Isaac.

Scholars debate whether Abraham took Keturah before or after the death of Sarah. There are great arguments for either option. They also debate whether "the concubines" mentioned here are only referring to Hagar and Keturah. There are also strong arguments here that could lead to either conclusion.

Abraham's Death and Burial

Intro) The Genesis record closes its account of Abraham's life with a brief account of his death. It is significant that Ishmael and Isaac do not only bury their father, but also (at least for the time) any hostility which may have come between them over the years.

For now, one of the most significant characters in the unfolding story of God's dealings with mankind is laid to rest.

Read Genesis 25:7-11

At the good ole age of 175, our first recorded patriarch dies. His sons, Isaac and Ishmael (who had come from the wilderness to grieve and bury his father), went and laid their father in the cave of Machpelah, in the field of Ephron, which Abraham had purchased earlier to bury Sarah. Abraham was a "friend of God," "father of the faithful," generous, unselfish, and a superb character (though he too had his flaws). We should be surely grateful for his life.

Now, with the death of Abraham, the mantle of the covenant promise fell upon Isaac, who dwelt at Beer Lahai Roi. This residence of Isaac was at the same well where Hagar had been greeted by the Angel of Jehovah and was refreshed after her expulsion from the household of Abraham.

The Families of Ishmael and Isaac

Intro) Ishmael is 89 years old when his father, Abraham, dies. He will live for another 48 years. Because the Genesis record will soon concentrate exclusively on the life of Isaac and his descendants, a final account of Ishmael and his sons is given at this point.

Read Genesis 25:12-28.

12-18) Ishmael was Abraham's oldest son whom he bore through Hagar, Sarah's maid. In this brief text we are given the names, in genealogical order, of the sons of Ishmael. We are informed of the twelve princes that descended from Ishmael. Through them the promise of God, recorded in chapter 17, verse 20, was fulfilled. This promise was that Ishmael would be a great nation and beget twelve princes. Ishmael lived 137 years, died, and was gathered to his people.

Intro to 19-28) With the death of Abraham, the Genesis record begins to provide increasing detail regarding the lives of Abraham's descendants, and events are recorded at briefer intervals. Where major events of the first 2,500 or so years have been chronicled as only a brief outline, the remainder of the Genesis record provides an in-depth look at Isaac's children and grandchildren. For the most part, the events speak for themselves. The people whose lives are recorded exhibit both the best and worst of human nature, typifying the moral struggles which encompass the human predicament and pointing up the need for a God who can lift mankind above its own circumstances.

The second of the great Hebrew patriarchs, Isaac, is somewhat overshadowed by his illustrious father and by his famous son, whom we will be introduced to in this lesson. Much of Isaac's life is included in the narratives about Abraham and Jacob, so material specifically devoted to Isaac is limited.

1. In the account of Abraham we see the birth and childhood of Isaac, his father's trial, and Isaac's marriage.
2. In material devoted to Jacob are recorded events of Isaac's old age and death.

The scene for the next 150 years is set when Rebekah gives birth to twins and is told, prophetically, that these two sons will be the fathers of nations which will in time struggle with each other for dominance. The account picks up immediately following the death of Isaac's father.

21) Isaac is devoted to Rebekah. He is also concerned about her inability to conceive, so he prays. As a result of that prayer, Rebekah became pregnant with not one, but two sons.

22-24) *If all is well* – These alarming movements must have meant something to her. So she wonders ... Why am I this way? Jehovah answers her question:

1. There are two nations = Two children
2. They will be separate nations.
3. One will be stronger than the other. This does not mean that one will be weak.
4. The older shall serve the younger – just the opposite of what would be anticipated.

25-26) When Esau was born, the account gave two specifics of his birth.

1. He was red – The Hebrew word for "red" is a form of Edom. Esau is also called Edom.
2. He was unusually hairy – His name, Esau, means "hairy".

Jacob is born while grabbing the heel of Esau.

1. The name, Jacob, means "one who takes by the heel" and "one who supplants".
2. In light of the prediction of vs. 23, the hand on the heel was taken as symbolic of the intention of the younger brother to replace his elder brother and secure his advantages.

Before Jacob and Esau were born, God knew the qualities of the two men and chose Jacob. He hinted this to Rebekah in verse 23. In the line of promise, all of Abraham's sons were eliminated except Isaac. Of Isaac's sons, only Jacob was chosen.

26) The text informs us that Isaac is 60 years old when his sons were born. This was 20 years following their marriage.

27-28) As Esau and Jacob grow into manhood, they take on individual characteristics and become favored.

1. Esau was a hunter, so Isaac loved him because he had a taste for wild game.
2. Jacob, who was a quiet man, was favored by Rebekah.

* Both were wrong to favor one child over the other!

Esau Sells His Birthright

Intro) An incident having extraordinary consequences is now recorded which not only gives insight into the character of each man, but also has important implications for the further descent of the people through whom God has chosen to reveal Himself.

Read Genesis 25:29-34.

29-34) Esau, as first-born son, had right, under usual circumstances, to the major portion of the inheritance and to the honor and privilege of continuance of the family name. In Abraham's line the birthright also involved major spiritual advantages of covenant. This important position was bartered from Esau by the crafty Jacob for a simple meal.

1. The famished hunter let the urgency of his hunger outweigh, in his mind, the great value of the birthright.
2. So that Esau would not later take back his bargain, Jacob has him swear an oath that would bind the agreement.
3. Because of this this event, Esau is a classic example of one who fails to evaluate properly the important and long-term things in life.

Note: Birthright – the double portion law has not been instituted yet. In fact verse 5 shows Isaac received all of the inheritance and the others received gifts (v. 6).

Genesis – Chapter 26

Isaac and Abimelech

Intro) As his two sons engage in fraternal conflict, Isaac himself experiences moral conflict in a series of situations which are amazingly parallel to situations experienced by his father, Abraham. It is interesting to note the influence of a parent and, in a more general sense, the cycles of human behavior which we can observe throughout history.

Read Genesis 26.

1-5) In the beginning of this text we see God reassuring Isaac of the covenant made to Abraham that, because of Abraham's complete obedience, will be passed along to Isaac. The implication of the statement by God is that Isaac, like Abraham, must be true and obedient to God's charge.

There were two admonitions:
1. Do not go down to Egypt
2. Stay in the land of the Philistines and Jehovah will bless him.

So far as the record goes, this (in these 5 verses) is the first appearance of God to Isaac since he was on Mount Moriah.

1) *There was a famine in the land* – This famine came nearly a hundred years after the one in Abraham's day.

4) *Multiply as the stars of heaven* – "Dust of the earth," "sands of the seashore," and "stars of heaven" are all metaphors of the "seed of Abraham."

5) *Because Abraham obeyed* – God's fulfillment of his promise to Abraham was here said to have been "because," that is, as a result of, Abraham's obedience. The sequence here is not that God saved Abraham, and then Abraham obeyed because God saved him, but that Abraham obeyed, and because he did so, God saved him and fulfilled his promise.

6-9) Soon after his discussion with God, Isaac falters and practices the same deception utilized by Abraham in Egypt and Gerar. So, due to famine, Isaac is looking to relocate. God informs Isaac to not go to Egypt, but to the place that He would show him. When the men of Gerar inquire about Isaac's wife, he lies, as did his father, and claims that she is his sister. Upon seeing Isaac caressing Rebekah, Abimelech rebukes Isaac for deceiving him. In spite of this deception, God continues to bless Isaac.

Note that Abimelech seems suspicious of Isaac's allegation that Rebekah was his sister, that he seems to have investigated personally, that he discovered them in the process of lovemaking, etc. All of that leads scholars to believe that Abimelech knew of the earlier event in the times of Abraham, and that he acted accordingly.

Abimelech was a dynastic title of early Philistine kings, leaving it unclear whether or not he was the same monarch who took Sarah. The time lapse makes it highly probable that the two were different kings.

Note: If we recognize the insecurity of the typical sojourner in many ancient Near Eastern societies, we can understand the fear of these patriarchs; nevertheless, these acts of deception reflect an occasional wavering of trust in the divine assurance of protection.

10-11) Abimelech hands down a well-deserved rebuke. He then charges the people to not touch Isaac or his wife lest they be put to death. Can you imagine today if people were so concerned about these matters?! A sense of guilt here shows that the morals of God have not been entirely forgotten.

12-18) Isaac keeps growing richer and richer. Because of Isaac's prosperity the Philistines envied him. This envy motivated the Philistines to stop up the wells and fill them with earth. This would cause the loss of much-needed water. Abimelech then expels Isaac from Gerar. Isaac's peaceable characteristics cause him to avoid further conflict with the herdsmen of Gerar and simply move his herds in search of other water sources. How long he stayed in that place is not stated; but the next scene finds him again near the home he left when he went unto Abimelech (Genesis 26:1). He gives tribute to his father Abraham by giving the wells the names that Abraham had previously given them.

19-20) After Isaac's servants find a well, contention arises with the herdsmen. Isaac is peaceable and moves on again.

21) Another well and another argument. Again Isaac is peaceable and moves on. Remember, Abraham was given the right to live in Abimelech's whole domain, and the envious Philistines were acting illegally by trying to prevent Isaac's use of their country. When disputes arose, Isaac resolved them by yielding and moving to another place, trusting Jehovah, rather than taking things into his own hands and engaging in armed conflict.

22) Finally, Isaac has reached a place with no quarreling.

23-25) Perhaps out of fear of the continued hostility of the Philistines, Isaac gave ground and went all the way to Beersheba. That he did the right thing in this was at once confirmed by a reassuring appearance of Jehovah to the patriarch the very same night he arrived there. The "Fear not!" from God Himself might indicate that fear had encroached upon Isaac's peace of mind.

26-31) At some point Abimelech recognizes Isaac's increasing power. Because of this increasing power, Abimelech seeks assurance that Isaac's power will not be turned against him.

27) *Why have you come to me* – Isaac was surprised, and spoke of Abimelech's having "sent him" away, making mention also of the obvious hatred of Abimelech and the Philistines for Isaac.

The covenant proposed to Isaac is a pact of non-aggression. This pact would certainly recognize Isaac's water rights, which were the matter of the most recent disputes. Isaac accepts the proposal and celebrates with a great feast, keeping his guests overnight.

32-33) God blesses them with water.

Such a progression of events must have been supremely satisfying to Isaac. Under pressure, and perhaps even fear, he moved to Beersheba. God appeared to him in a comforting and encouraging vision that same night. Then Abimelech unexpectedly visited him, requesting a treaty of peace. The treaty was celebrated with a great feast. The king departed in peace. The servants who had been digging a well, came that very day and reported that they had found water. It was an occasion to be memorialized. The well is named "Beersheba." In fact, this well is still in existence.

34-35) Here we get a brief account of Esau marrying two of the local Hittite women. These women are somewhat of a burden to Isaac and Rebekah. We can remember the concern that Abraham had for Isaac when it came to these people. This may very well show us a lack of spiritual values or concern on the part of Esau.

Genesis – Chapter 27

Isaac Blesses Jacob

Intro) Beginning with this chapter and throughout the rest of Genesis, the life, posterity, and activities of Jacob are the invariable theme. Following this emphasis, he takes his place as "The Israel" of God; he was the father of the Twelve Tribes of Israel, and remained at the head of the chosen family until they were favorably settled in Egypt, and where they would, in time, become the mighty nation that God had foretold in his promises to Abraham and Isaac.

In several respects the differences and difficulties between Jacob and Esau are not unlike that between Cain and Abel centuries earlier. Like their predecessors, Jacob and Esau have different occupations, temperament, and moral characteristics. Esau, like Cain, appears to be the rebellious sort, as may be demonstrated by his marriages to two women from among the local heathen population.

But Jacob himself is not without fault. Prompted by his mother's scheming, Jacob conspires with Rebekah to deceive Isaac, who, in his old age, wishes to bestow a special blessing upon his own favorite son, Esau.

Read Genesis 27:1-29.

1-4) Believing death is near, Isaac instructs Esau to hunt some wild game and prepare a meal for him. You'll remember, this is what made Esau the "favorite" in the eyes of Isaac. Isaac promises to bless Esau following the meal.

5-12) Overhearing this conversation, Rebekah plots to prepare a similar meal, disguise Jacob to resemble Esau, and send him in to Isaac. Jacob objects to his mother's crafty plan, not on the basis of ethical conviction, but out of fear of being caught and, as a result, cursed.

13) *Let your curse be on me* – This impromptu prayer of Rebekah was a disaster, for she did indeed that day suffer the loss of her beloved Jacob and never saw him anymore. Little did she realize that her death would come before he could return. Indeed the curse did fall upon her.

13-17) To avoid getting caught, Jacob dresses in Esau's best garments. These would have the smell of Isaac's favorite son Esau. Jacob also puts on the skins of the kid goats. These would resemble the rough, hairy skin of Esau. The meal prepared would resemble the taste of the prepared kill. Rebekah thinks of every detail and arranges the deception so that the senses of touch, taste, and smell would all support Jacob in his appearance before Isaac.

Rebekah seems unwilling to trust the Lord's ability to fulfill His prediction given earlier, and instead resorted to unethical measure of deceit. Remember what the Lord had told her in 25:23? This is somewhat similar to Sarah's introducing Abraham to Hagar. It seems that Rebekah is trying to assist God in fulfilling His earlier prediction. Unfortunately, it will only cause trouble.

18-20) Jacob carries out the plan by going to Isaac pretending to be Esau. Not only is Jacob lying with his actions but now will lie with his words as well. Of interest here are the number of falsehoods attributable to Jacob:

1. He said, "I am your first-born."
2. "I have brought the venison, as you commanded."
3. "I did it so quickly because your God' gave me good speed."
4. He wore Esau's clothes.
5. He wore goat hair on his neck and hands.
6. He answered his father's specific question, "Art thou Esau," by saying, "I am."
7. He feigned the irreligion of Esau – It is curious that Jacob referred to Jehovah in this episode as "your God," thus answering the question after the manner of the irreligious Esau, who from this appears as one who had renounced all faith in God for himself.

21-29) The deception is complete. Jacob receives the blessing and the prophecy of his future.

26) *Kiss me, my son* – The kiss appears here for the first time as the token of true love and deep affection. But we are unable to miss that it is a kiss of deceit on the part of Jacob.

29) *And nations bow down to you* – All of the thirty-two kingdoms of Canaan were conquered, subdued, and driven out of Palestine by the posterity of Jacob, as prophesied here; but there is a remote and greater fulfillment also which took place in Christ as manifested on earth in his Church. The ancient prophets expanded on this prophecy by affirming that, "For the nation and kingdom which will not serve you shall perish, and those nations shall be utterly ruined ... (they) shall come bowing to you" (Isaiah 60:12, 14). The fulfillment of this came when the Gentiles bowed before the feet of Christ.

Esau's Lost Hope

Read Genesis 27:30-40.

30-40) As Jacob exits, after receiving Isaac's blessing, Esau enters ready for his blessing. When he learns of Jacob's acts, Esau weeps out of anger and frustration and begs his father to bless him too. Isaac responds by telling him that he and his descendants will live by the sword and serve his brother for a time. This blessing was not even a pale copy of the one given to Jacob.

The blessing of Esau did allow one small hope, that, on occasions, Edom would be able to throw off the yoke of Israel. An example of this was in the reign of Joram, king of Judah (2 Kings 8:20-22; 2 Chronicles 21:8-10). Another occasion is mentioned in the Book of Obadiah. Still another, perhaps, is seen in the fact that Herod the Great was descended from Esau; and he was ruling Israel ruthlessly in the days of Christ.

Jacob Escapes from Esau

Read Genesis 27:41-46.

41) So Esau hated his brother and vowed to kill him following the death of their father Isaac.

42-45) It appears that Esau told someone of his intent to kill Jacob, and the word reached Rebekah. Rebekah, fearing for Jacob's life, urges him to flee to her hometown of Haran in Mesopotamia.

46) Here, Rebekah expresses concern about the future of Jacob if he were to marry into the wrong family. It appears that she might, even here, have been less than candid with Isaac. There's not a word here of the knowledge that Rebekah had regarding Esau's intention of killing Jacob, nor of the previous decision Rebekah had already made to send Jacob to her brother's home in Haran. While what she said was most certainly the truth, it was far from all of the truth. Despite this lack of candor, it is hard to fault Rebekah for the skilled manner in which she prevailed with Isaac. We will continue with that in the next chapter.

Although the motivations of the participants in this drama are not always clear, it appears that none of the parties in this tragedy were entirely free from guilt.

- Isaac does not seem to have given adequate attention to the Lord's prediction to Rebekah. Surely he would have learned about it from her.
- Esau appears to have desired to reverse, to some extent, the agreement that he had previously made regarding his birthright.
- Rebekah and Jacob practiced deception in order to secure for Jacob the blessing that Isaac had intended for Esau.
- As a result of this deception, the entire family suffered distrust, hostility, and the heartaches of long separation. Jacob left home, and Rebekah, as far as the record says, never saw him anymore. Esau was further estranged.

Genesis – Chapter 28

Jacob escapes from Esau Cont'd

Intro) As a result of Esau's threat, Jacob follows his mother's suggestion, and patriarchal mandate, and leaves for Haran, the region Rebekah once called home. Isaac seems to have reconciled himself to the fact that it is Jacob through whom God's promises to Abraham will be fulfilled, so he sends Jacob away with his blessing. To this Esau reacts with typical rebellion.

Read Genesis 28:1-5.

1-5) Isaac, in response to Rebekah's fear of Jacob's marrying a woman from the local Canaanites, gives Jacob his blessing and sends him away to find an adequate wife.

The reason behind Jacob's being commanded to take a wife from among the daughters of Laban lay in the fact that it was imperative that the head of the chosen nation be relieved of the burden of paganism in his own family.

Note: The usual calculation for the age of Jacob at this time is 77 years, although another method of calculating his age makes it about 57. If the first is correct, then Ishmael had been dead fourteen years when Isaac commanded Jacob to go to the house of Bethuel. If the second calculation is allowed, Ishmael still lived and would not have died until six years later. The statement that "Esau went to Ishmael" (Genesis 28:9), inferring that Ishmael was alive at the time of the events of this chapter, definitely favors the lower calculations of 57 for the age of Jacob. The Bible here says nothing whatever about anyone's age, and human deductions are subject to all kinds of errors.

Esau Marries Mahalath

Read Genesis 28:6-9.

6-9) Now Esau, realizing that his Canaanite wives are a source of grief for his parents, marries Mahalath, daughter of Ishmael.

Jacob's Vow at Bethel

Intro) The highlight of this chapter, of course, is Jacob's vision of the ladder reaching to heaven, the whole chapter being built around that event.

Read Genesis 28:10-22.

10-12) As Jacob is on his journey, he stops for the night to sleep. He then has a dream. A dream in general, such as Jacob's, was often a vehicle for revelation. During this dream, Jacob sees angels ascending and descending upon a ladder, or stairway, reaching from earth to heaven. This ladder is thought by many to be a representation of Christ. Using John 1:51 as reference it may seem that this ladder was a hint that this would all culminate into a "bridge" connecting heaven and earth, and filling the gap. The entire scene that is visualized in this dream seems to symbolize communion between heaven and earth.

13-15) God reaffirms that it will indeed be Jacob through whose descendants the promise given to Abraham will be fulfilled. The transfer of the birthright has now been validated in heaven, with God Himself giving His assurance to Jacob. The promise of many descendants made to Abraham and Isaac is confirmed for Jacob. The crucial "blessing for all nations," the Messianic element, is confirmed for Jacob by God as Isaac had hoped in verse 4. Like Abraham and Isaac before him, Jacob is assured of the Lord's protection. All of these statements constitute a renewal/confirmation of the Abrahamic covenant with Jacob, Abraham's grandson.

Note: There are many great teachings that are inherent in this dream. Here are a few:

- The continual interest of God in His human creation is evident. Earth is not isolated from God or from heaven. There is a line of communication. Countless angels are busy as divine servants, "ministering for those who will inherit salvation" (Hebrews 1:14).
- The omnipresence of God, called also His ubiquitousness, was also shown in this dream. Jacob was away from home, in a strange land, and fleeing from the wrath of a brother, but one cannot flee beyond the watchful eye of the Lord. No more could Jacob than Jonah, run away from God. Every man must discover (sooner or later) that "Surely God is in this place (every place)," whether men know it or not.
- The ladder is also a type of the Lord Jesus Christ. The ladder was "the way" between earth and heaven; and Christ affirmed that He is indeed "the Way" (John 14:6); and, as Jacob saw the angels of God ascending and descending upon that ladder, Jesus affirmed to Nathaniel that he would "see angels ascending and descending upon the Son of Man" (John 1:51). The ladder is therefore a perfect representation of Christ in that in Him, God came down to men, and in Him men themselves may go up to God and be in heaven with him forever. Christ is the only avenue of communication between God and men (1 Timothy 2:5), just as this ladder in the dream was the only way to God's presence. To miss this significance of the ladder is to lose the most important thing in the chapter.

16-19) When Jacob woke up he was filled with profound reverence as he realized that the Lord has appeared to him. Anywhere that God made an appearance was regarded as a special place of worship. He refers to the place as the "house of God" and the "gate of heaven." This most likely conveyed the idea that this was a place where God meets man. Jacob sets up his headrest, anoints it (an act of worship), and calls the place Bethel, which means "house of God."

20-22) Jacob makes a vow to God. Some say that Jacob is bargaining with God. That he will serve God ONLY IF God protects and provides for him. Others say that, due to the custom language, Jacob will serve God BECAUSE God will protect and provide for him. Even though we have seen Jacob use such bargaining techniques before, I tend to lean toward the latter. You can decide which way you lean.

In addition to serving God, Jacob vows to give a tenth of all that God gives him, back to God.

Note: Although as a man of faith Jacob was not always faithful, he was from that day forward pointed in the right direction spiritually as a result of his profound encounter with God at Bethel.

Genesis – Chapter 29

Jacob Meets Rachel

Intro) As he returns to his mother's country, Jacob meets her brother Laban and agrees to work for him in exchange for his daughter Rachel. But Laban deceives Jacob, giving him his older daughter, Leah, instead of Rachel. Ultimately Jacob gets both Leah and Rachel, but Laban's deception surely must have reminded Jacob of his own deception which forced his flight to Haran in the first place.

Read Genesis 29:1-14.

1-3) Completing his journey to northern Mesopotamia, where Haran is located, Jacob arrives at a well where he meets Rachel, Laban's daughter. Some scholars believe that this could be the same well where the servant of Abraham met Rebekah years earlier. This is certainly a possibility considering this was in the same vicinity. The text does not tell us that specifically. The well seemed to be a common watering hole used by a number of shepherds, the entrance being kept by the placement of a heavy stone. The rolling of the stone served to keep the stored up water from evaporating as well as to maintain control over the amount of water used and possibly as a safety precaution.

4-7) Jacob, once he notices Rachel coming with the sheep, seems to try to get rid of the kinsmen who had arrived earlier, maybe desiring a private interview with Rachel.

8-10) As Rachel arrives, Jacob removes the stones and waters the flock of Laban. Jacob may have done this to simply greet Rachel with courtesy, knowing she was Laban's daughter.

11-12) Jacob wept with joy and lifted his voice once he realized that he had been aided in such a swift way on his journey. He then tells Rachel who he is. Rachel, upon learning of Jacob's relation, ran and told her father.

13-14) Laban, upon learning of Jacob's presence and relation, ran back to meet him and greeted him with an embrace and a kiss. Laban then invites Jacob to stay with them.

13) *He told Laban all these things* – This probably refers to being sent back by his parents to find a suitable wife, the confirmation of the covenant by God, and the meeting between Rachel and Jacob at the well.

Jacob Marries Leah and Rachel

Read Genesis 29:15-30.

15-21) During the first month of Jacob's stay, he evidently worked for Laban and demonstrated his competence. Laban, believing that Jacob should not work for free, asks Jacob to suggest a wage to him. Jacob wishes to receive Rachel, Laban's younger daughter, in exchange for seven years of service. At the completion of his service, Jacob went to Laban and requested his bride.

22-25) Laban gathered all the men together and prepared a feast. This feast, which lasted seven days, was often part of a marriage celebration. On the eve of the wedding, Laban secretly substitutes Leah, his oldest daughter, for Rachel.

- The bride was veiled from the time the feasting began until the marriage union was consummated.
- This, plus the fact that consummation in the wedding tent took place at night, explains how the deception was possible without detection.
- Jacob, the deceiver of Isaac, meets another deceiver. In the substitution of Leah, Laban begins to be seen in his true character as a shrewd and crafty trickster.

26-27) Laban gives Jacob a seemingly valid excuse for his acts, informing him that the custom did not allow for the younger daughter to be given in marriage prior to the oldest daughter.

- There was in fact such a custom among the Indians, Egyptians, and other countries, and it was possible that Laban had heard of these customs. However, there is no evidence that any customs prevailed in this vicinity.
- If this was in fact the custom of the area, a more honorable man would have explained the custom to Jacob prior to making the original bargain.
- Either way, whether or not this custom was in place, Laban did not follow through with the original agreement.
- We are also left to wonder what role Rachel played in this deceitful act. It seems that this would have not been possible without her knowledge and/or consent. But we are only left to speculate.

28-30) Once Jacob fulfills the marriage agreement to Leah, he is given Rachel also along with the expectation of his working another seven years for Laban. This particular situation is somewhat different than the first agreement. In this case, Jacob is given Rachel prior to his completing the seven years of labor. Jacob marries Rachel and clearly loves her more than Leah.

* Seeds of trouble – Jacob has two wives and loves Rachel more than Leah.

Note: The text tells us that Leah's eyes were delicate. Most believe this to mean that they were weak, that she may have lacked normal vision. However, others say that her principal beauty laid in the luster and softness of her beautiful eyes.

The Children of Jacob

Read Genesis 29:31-35.

31-35) The Lord saw that Leah was unloved, so He opened her womb; but Rachel was barren. Some translations use the term "hated" here. The idea given is that Leah was not loved as much as Rachel. The word "hated" indicates less affection or less devotion; it does not indicate positive hatred (cf. Luke 14:26).

Born to Leah here: Reuben, Simeon, Levi, and Judah.

Genesis – Chapter 30

The Children of Jacob Cont'd

Intro) Just the names of these sons of Jacob constitute as eloquent and convincing a commentary on his polygamous household as any that could be written. The bitter, unending rivalry between Rachel and Leah; Rachel was sitting like a queen in the middle and doling out to the other women when they might lie with Jacob; her bitterness that she had no children; her desperate prayer, "Give me children, or I die"; Leah's frustration that Jacob never took her into his heart; What a tragic household that was!

Read Genesis 30:1-24.

1-4) When Rachel saw that she bore Jacob no children, she envied her sister Leah. Rachel gives Jacob her maidservant, Bilhah, so that she may have children through her. In keeping with the custom that we discussed in chapter 16 regarding Sarai and Hagar, Rachel plans to claim as legally hers by adoption any sons borne by Bilhah.

5-8) Bilhah conceived and bore two sons.

1. Dan
2. Naphtali

9-13) When Leah saw that she had stopped bearing, she gave Jacob her maidservant, Zilpah. She bore him two sons.

1. Gad
2. Asher

14-16) Reuben, while out in a wheat field, found some mandrakes and brought them to his mother Leah. Perhaps, when Rachel saw Reuben with the mandrakes, she supposed that, at last, she had found out Leah's secret for bearing children.

* The mandrake was an herb that gave berries resembling a yellow plum. It also had a fleshy root and was commonly regarded in ancient superstition as having aphrodisiac and fertility-producing qualities (because of this, they were also called "love apples").

When Leah is asked for some of her son's mandrakes, she lashes out at Rachel who, despite her barrenness, has continued to receive the bulk of Jacob's attention. At this point Jacob almost appears to be a pawn between the two women who is passed from one to the other in a bargain for these mandrakes. Jacob went to Leah, as a result of this bargain.

17-21) Leah, in all, gave birth to six sons by Jacob. She made each of their names symbolic of her gratitude and hope.

1. Reuben
2. Simeon
3. Levi
4. Judah

5. Issachar
6. Zebulun

Leah, along with six sons, bore Jacob a daughter whom they named Dinah. Whether Jacob had more than one daughter is not known. Dinah is the only one mentioned here.

22-24) Finally, God remembered Rachel, opened her womb, and she bore Joseph.

Note: This account is not an endorsement by God for the acts that took place. However, it shows us that God has a plan and He uses human beings, just as they are, to serve His purpose.

Jacob's Agreement With Laban

Sometime after Joseph is born, Jacob decides to return to Canaan. However, he agrees with Laban on appropriate wages to continue his service. Jacob devises a scheme to increase the flocks which are rightfully his by their agreement. Apparently Jacob held an early belief that whatever objects sheep happen to view while mating will affect the genetic characteristics of their young.

Read Genesis 30:25-43.

25-28) With his accounts squared with Laban, Jacob asks to leave and take his family with him. Laban recognizes that Jacob's faithful service has satisfied all demands of the earlier contracts between them. Both Jacob and Laban recognize that Laban's extraordinary prosperity has been due to God's blessing Jacob. So Laban desires to keep the competent foreman who has brought him much prosperity, and therefore he asks for Jacob's demands for continued service.

29-33) Jacob agrees to continue working for Laban under certain conditions. Jacob asks that Laban give him all the speckled and spotted sheep, and all the brown ones among the lambs, and the spotted and speckled among the goats.

- Sheep were ordinarily white and goats were normally black or dark-colored.
- Jacob simply asked for the animals which were exceptions to the usual coloring of these particular breeds.
- Under normal circumstances, these would not be very numerous.
- The thought seems that, after this group of animals has been removed from the flock, similar animals born in the future will belong to Jacob.

Laban will also be able to continuously check on Jacob's adherence to the agreement because all of Jacob's animals will be colored in this manner. Laban agrees with the conditions that Jacob suggested.

34-36) The text states here that *"he removed that day the male goats that were speckled and spotted, all the female goats that were speckled and spotted, every one that had some white in it, and all the brown ones among the lambs, and gave them into the hand of his sons. Then he put three days' journey between himself and Jacob, and Jacob fed the rest of Laban's flocks."* – This text is viewed in different ways by different Bible scholars. The variances are notable even though the subject matter is relatively unimportant.

- One source stated that Laban took the sheep out of the flocks because he did not trust Jacob to honestly do so.
- One stated that Laban took these flocks without Jacob's knowledge of it in order to try to deceive Jacob. He then hid them.
- Another stated that Laban separated and moved the stock so they could not breed more like themselves in the pure flock.
- Yet another stated that it was Jacob who took the flocks, gave them to his sons, and put the distance between them and Laban out of his distrust of Laban.

I guess I can see the reasoning behind some of these opinions. However, I do not see how the suggestion is made that Jacob took the flocks. The fact is that we are not given the motives behind these actions. We are simply given the facts and we must be careful how we input our opinions.

37-43) It seems Jacob sought to use selective breeding in his favor. Than he tried to influence the breeding of the flocks. Maybe he thought that by facing the normal-colored animals toward the unusual-colored animals while they conceived, they would breed unusual-colored animals. Jacob also placed the rods in front of the stronger livestock and held it back from the feeble livestock. We find out through the text that Jacob then becomes extremely prosperous. His methods "appear" to be working.

* It must be noted that this all could have possibly been a command of God, though not mentioned specifically in the text. We simply cannot completely discount that possibility.

Later, Jacob learned that his success was due, not to his ingenious and somewhat questionable devices, but rather to God's providential care which prevented Laban from defrauding him.

Genesis – Chapter 31

Jacob Flees From Laban

Intro) If there is one lapse in moral character which besets early man – including God's special people – it is dishonesty and trickery. Fearful that Laban might not let him leave, Jacob secretly steals away with his family and flocks. To make matters worse, Rachel takes some household gods belonging to her father and later covers up her theft by lying to him. After Jacob and Laban exchange hostile accusations, they resolve their differences by establishing a mutual treaty of peace.

In all the dealings between Jacob and Laban, and again in the reprehensible conduct of Rachel, there is a reminder that God can work His will even through men and women who share in the frailties of moral character.

Read Genesis 31:1-21.

1-6) The beginning of the text gives us the three reasons why Jacob is now choosing to leave Laban for sure.

1. Jacob had heard the hostile words of Laban's sons, this was envy due to Jacob's prosperity.
2. Also, Jacob notices that trouble is brewing as Laban's countenance toward him is now unfavorable.
3. Finally, the Lord tells Jacob to, "Return to the land of your father and grandfather."

Jacob tells Rachel and Leah of God's command and begins to remind them of their father's deceit.

7) Jacob feels that Laban has deceived him. The text says that the wages for Jacob were changed 10 times. Some scholars take this literally. Others say that this is idiomatic for something done "repeatedly." No matter what Laban did, every change turned out to the benefit of Jacob. And Jacob recognizes that he has been under God's protective care during these trying times.

8-13) Here we see what could be examples of Laban's altering the wages of Jacob. Remember that Jacob and Laban had agreed to terms in which all speckled, spotted, and striped animals along with the black sheep would be given to Jacob in return for his work.

- Verse 8 says, *"If he said thus, 'The speckled shall be your wages,' then all the flocks bore speckled."*
- Verse 8 continues, *"And if he said thus, 'the streaked shall be your wages,' then all the flocks bore streaked."*

It seems that Laban agreed to the original terms, was not happy with the results, then changed the terms to further limit the growth of Jacob's increase. And it seems that he did this a number of times. However, these changes did not alter God's role and His plan for Jacob. Jacob's herds continued to increase. Through the dream, Jacob learns that his success has been due to God's providence.

14-16) Informed of their father's trickery, and of the divine message that Jacob has received, Rachel and Leah, who seem to be angry with their father because of his dealings with them, agree to leave their homeland to return with their husband to Canaan. Laban had failed to keep the respect of his daughters because of the shameful way he dealt with them.

- The brides refer to the bridal price which was paid by Jacob in labor to Laban so that he could marry them.
- Under normal circumstances, at least part of the bridal payment was given to the bride as a dowry or personal holding.
- Laban, however, accepted Jacob's payment and did not provide a gift or dowry for his daughters. Rachel and Leah consider themselves "sold".
- So the thought in the text may be, "Although our father has shown he will give us no inheritance, God has provided for us this property."
- Jacob's wives encourage him to follow what God told him to do.

Every sign Jacob was getting told him that it was time for him to return to Canaan.

- From Laban's sons (v. 1)
- From Laban (v. 2)
- From God (v. 3)
- From his wives (v. 14-16)

17-21) Jacob and his family do not tell Laban of their departure, instead, they flee. And as his family, and his flocks depart, Rachel steals the household gods of Laban. These must have been some sort of small portable idol. (They were small enough to place in a camel's saddle and sit on unnoticeably.)

Why did Rachel steal the idols (Teraphim)?

- The Nuzu tablets, excavated in 1930, stated that, "The teraphim were associated with the inheritance and property rights of the owner." It could have been possible that Rachel supposed her possession of these would help to validate the legitimacy of her husband's title to the flocks and herds that he acquired while serving Laban.
- Another possibility is that she may have stolen them under the belief that they would provide her protection and blessing.
- She may have just wanted to have something tangible to worship on the long journey ahead.
- One suggestion is that she took them in order to keep her father from worshipping them.
- Whatever the reason, we can see that Rachel is not free of her pagan background.

Laban Pursues Jacob

Read Genesis 31:22-42.

22-24) Laban learns, after three days, that Jacob and his entire camp have left without informing him and evidently have stolen the family idols. Laban rides with his men to overtake Jacob. As patriarchal head, Laban could have brought legal charges and, in company with his men, he might have committed violence. But Laban, who worships other gods, has been warned by the true God against harming Jacob.

24) *Be careful that you speak to Jacob neither good nor bad* – "anything"- He is not to try to influence Jacob to return or, do anything of bitter reproach.

25-30) Laban confronts Jacob by asking two questions, "Why did you slip away secretly? ... Why have you stolen my household gods?" Laban seems to be giving the "hurt-feelings" approach.

31) Jacob replies that is was ultimately Laban's dishonesty and unrighteousness that caused him to leave. He left secretly because of fear.

32) Jacob insists that he did not steal Laban's gods. In fact, Jacob was so sure of their innocence that he threatened the life of the guilty party if the gods were found. Jacob's patriarchal authority over his family allowed for this penalty for theft.

33-42) After Laban is unable to present the stolen possessions to Jacob, we begin to see the frustration of Jacob burst forth following 20 years of mistreatment. Jacob insists that he went beyond the legal requirements of a shepherd. These would have granted him an occasional ram for food. They also would have relieved him of responsibility for animals torn by wild beasts (especially if evidence was presented). Jacob's language reflects the hardships of shepherd life as sleep fled from his eyes. He spent many sleepless nights protecting the flocks from predatory beasts. Now he is being accused of theft of a pagan god.

Note: It is worthy here to mention how Jacob gives the credit of his prosperity and protection to God. But he also shows how God had protected the wealth and well-being of Laban during this time.

Laban's Covenant with Jacob

Read Genesis 31:43-55.

43-44) Despite the contracts of the past, Laban pretends to have legal claim to Jacob's family and herds. Laban, as a result, pretends that his relinquishing the daughters and children is an act of generosity and love. It seems as if Laban may be trying to save face before his kinsmen, whom he had assembled to pursue Jacob as though Jacob were in the wrong.

45-53) A treaty of peace was agreed to by both men. The heap of stones may very well have symbolized the witness of God over the actions of the parties involved in this covenant. Boundary markers were placed between Laban and Jacob not to be crossed by the other for harm. It is evident that the covenant meant two different things to the participants. To Jacob, it was a victory; to Laban it was a face-saving device.

It seems this covenant arose out of mutual suspicion and sought protection not for the other but for each one from the other's malice. Laban also added some stipulations of his own designed to protect his daughters.

54-55) Jacob, following the peace agreement between himself and Laban, offered a sacrifice in gratitude to God. Laban arose the next morning, kissed and blessed his sons and daughters, then departed.

Note: We are only left to contemplate what might have happened had Laban actually found the stolen gods. Would Jacob have really handed his beloved Rachel over to her father to be put to death? Would Laban have executed such a penalty upon her?

Note: Jacob had left Canaan 20 years earlier, alone and empty-handed. He was now returning as head of a family and was rich in flocks, herds, and servants. God had kept His promise to Jacob.

Genesis – Chapter 32

Esau comes to meet Jacob

Intro) Realizing that he is going to pass through territory occupied by Esau, and apprehensive about the threat under which he had left Canaan, Jacob makes careful preparation in anticipation of encountering Esau. While he waits in uncertainty, Jacob is found rather mysteriously wrestling with God. In some way God presents Himself to Jacob, maybe even as a human being.

As Jacob leaves on his journey from Gilead to Canaan, he is met by messengers from God who give renewed assurance that God will be with him on his journey.

Read Genesis 32:1-21.

1-5) No sooner were his fears concerning Laban removed than Jacob had to face the prospect of meeting Esau, who had been plotting murder against him when they parted. However, angels reinforced to Jacob the divine promise of protection that was made at Bethel. Reassured by the angels, Jacob took the initiative in his projected confrontation with Esau. He sent a message, which is a model of humility, making clear that he desired reconciliation and peace upon his return.

6-8) The messengers return with some terrifying news for Jacob: Esau is coming with 400 men to meet Jacob.

1. Some scholars assume that these men were armed.
    a. Isaac had foretold that Esau would live "by the sword."
    b. Esau had gathered what were most likely fighting men.
    c. Jacob feared Esau might be bringing his many men to do violence. Cf. Genesis 27:42-45. Remember, when Jacob left home, his mother Rebekah had promised to send word when Esau's anger had cooled; but no word ever came. So Jacob feared the worst.
2. The problem with this is that there is no mention of their being armed.
    a. Esau's hostility had apparently vanished.
    b. That group of 400 men appeared to have no hostile intention.
3. These men may have been brought to help Jacob with his move.
4. They may have been brought along to provide a display of Esau's own success.
5. The fact is that we don't really know the reason behind Esau's bringing these men, but we are safe to conclude, by the following actions of Esau, that it was not to fight.

Esau had apparently forgiven Jacob (we will see this later) and probably longed to see him. Of course, as we have noticed, Jacob did not know that. So Jacob divides his people into two groups. If one is attacked, the other may flee.

9-12) Jacob prayed one of the greatest prayers of his life, consisting of several parts.

1. An invocation (v. 9)
2. His confession of unworthiness (v. 10)
3. Thanksgiving (v. 10)

4. Petition (v. 11)
5. An appeal to the divine faithfulness (v. 12)

* Jacob knew that if Esau still had revenge in his heart, Jacob's wives and children would suffer with him. Therefore he includes them in his prayer.

13-21) Fearing the wrath of Esau, Jacob sends generous gifts before him to possibly win Esau over. There were over 500 animals, and he arranged them in such a way that would emphasize the magnitude of the gifts and increase their effectiveness. It appears that none of the drove captains knew that he was being followed by another drove, and he was instructed to say, "Jacob is behind us." This arrangement may have kept a possible loose-tongued servant from revealing the full extent of the gift, which he would not know until Jacob appeared.

Wrestling With God

Read Genesis 32:22-32.

24-29) These verses give an account of a struggle, or perhaps a spiritual awakening on the part of Jacob. As he is waiting alone by the Jabbok River during the night, a "man" comes and wrestles with him until dawn. There are certainly different opinions and understandings of this event.

1. Some say that Jacob may have been engaged in prayer when the so called "man" encountered him.
2. Some allege that Jacob wrestled with a "local deity," one of the pagan river gods trying to prevent anyone from crossing the river.
3. Another scholar states that Jacob wrestled not with an angel but with his brother, Esau.
4. Some even hold that it was a struggle with a demon of some kind.
5. And yet others believe that it was some sort of dream.
6. Some take the text for what it is and concludes that this was real hand-to-hand combat.
7. Notice Hosea 12:3-5.

In verses 24 the assailant is called "a man," so the idea that God had assumed a human form is certainly not out of the question. The reality is that the plain meaning of this text is nearly, if not completely, impossible for modern man to comprehend or rationalize. Therefore, we must really be careful not to force the scripture to say something that it doesn't.

28-29) The scripture says that Jacob maintains the upper hand and God changes his name from Jacob to Israel. He was defeated and powerless to continue, but he clung to God and would not let go until he received the blessing. It is written that he "prevailed"; but how? He won by surrender, by confessing his unworthiness in the admission of his name (Heel-catcher), and by pleading for the blessing which could come only from the grace of God. He triumphed the same way that saints of all ages have, by clinging to the Lord and never letting go.

30-32) Jacob is touched on the socket of his hip and it is taken out of joint. Following this event, he will never walk the same again. He calls the place Peniel, meaning "face of God." God is a spirit being which no physical eye can behold. A Divine Being could only be seen by man if he manifested himself in some material form. This is how Moses saw him. This is how Jacob saw God "face to face."

Genesis – Chapter 33

Jacob and Esau Meet

Read Genesis 33:1-17.

1-2) Jacob rearranges his family into the order in which he wants Esau to meet them. Notice the order of least importance:

1. The handmaidens and their children first
2. Leah and her children next
3. Rachel and Joseph last.
4. But Jacob leads them all.

What was the reason for Jacob's arrangement of these divisions in his family, divisions that surely separated them in the order of his love for them? Two reasons have been suggested:

1. He did this to provide greater safety for Rachel and Joseph
2. He had in mind the order of their being presented to Esau, intending to present them in ascending climactic order.

Either reason, or both, might easily have motivated Jacob's action.

3) As Jacob approaches Esau he bows 7 times. This was a sign of total submission. The Tel el-Amarna tablets, dated in the 14th century B.C., record that "One approaching a king always bowed seven times in so doing."

4-7) To Jacob's relief, Esau embraces and kisses him. And soon they are both weeping for joy. The hatred of the past seems buried and forgotten. Esau sees the women and children and inquires to whom they belong. When Jacob left he was unmarried. So he naturally asks his question. Jacob gives God the credit for having graciously given him these.

8-11) The reason Jacob so urgently pressed his gift upon Esau was that, If Esau had refused to accept it, Jacob would never have been in peace. The refusal to accept a gift means permanent enmity. The gift was a token of reconciliation and everlasting peace. It healed the wound and repaired the breach.

12) Esau offers to lead them the rest of the way home.

13-14) Jacob, as a good shepherd and father, wants to take his time so as not to injure the livestock or children

15) Jacob rejects Esau's offer of a guard party. The offer of an escort by Esau was probably in good faith, but it probably would have been an embarrassment to Jacob.

Note: The steps that each brother took in the reconciliation:

JACOB:

1. he bowed before him seven times (Genesis 33:3);
2. he called himself Esau's servant twice (Genesis 33:5,14);
3. referred to Esau as his "lord" four times (Genesis 33:8,13,14);
4. dispatched ahead of time a most impressive present;
5. insisted that Esau keep it (Genesis 33:8-11); and
6. declared that seeing Esau's face was like seeing the face of God (Genesis 33:10).

ESAU:

1. came with a company to welcome Jacob;
2. ran to meet him;
3. embraced him;
4. fell on his neck;
5. kissed him;
6. invited Jacob to keep the present;
7. offered to accompany him;
8. offered to leave a guard to protect him;
9. addressed him as "my brother" (Genesis 33:9); and
10. graciously accepted the present, which in the customs of the day amounted to a pact of friendship.

Jacob Comes to Canaan

Read Genesis 33:18-20.

18-20) The final verses of this chapter speak of this patriarch's entry into Canaan, to the city of Shechem, where he purchased property, built a house, and apparently intended to stay a long time. Here Jacob built an altar to the Lord, thus following in the steps of Abraham, who built an altar wherever he went. The name of it is also significant, meaning, "mighty is the God of Israel," or "God is the God of Israel," for this is the first time that the name "Israel" was used after God gave it.

Conclusion: Jacob formally acknowledges and worships God, not only as the God who led his fathers, but more personally as the God who cares for him.

Genesis – Chapter 34

The Dinah Incident

Intro) As Jacob and his family come again into Canaan, his daughter, Dinah, becomes a central character in a story of violence turned into love, followed by treachery and revenge. The other main characters are Shechem, the local prince; Hamor, his father; and Simeon and Levi, two of Dinah's brothers.

Read Genesis 34.

1-10) The age of Dinah here is not known for certain, however, she was very young, probably 13-15. We are told here that she was the daughter of Jacob by Leah. Of all the children of Jacob mentioned in the text, Dinah is the only girl identified by name, and that was because of the tragic events of this chapter and the effects these events had on some of his sons.

The prince of the country, Shechem, saw Dinah, took her and lay with her, and violated her. And the drift of the chapter seems to indicate that Shechem raped Dinah against her will and forced her to live in his house. The very words that are used in the text, by definition, mean that:

1. An irresistible force was used.
2. That Dinah was humbled.
3. That Dinah was defiled.

Some commentators, though, are of the opinion that Dinah was rebellious and, as a result of her actions, may have encouraged Shechem. If that is the case, and we don't know that it is, Shechem was clearly out of line because of Dinah's age alone. (If a 13 year old student seduces an adult teacher today, does that make the teacher's sexual involvement acceptable?)

You may also notice that Shechem never shows any regret or regard to the wrong that he had done. There was no word of sorrow, no word of repentance, no word of seeking forgiveness. There was no admission whatever that any wrong was done by Shechem. The fact of the matter is that this act may not have been so severe in the eyes of these people. The standards here are noticeably different than those of Jacob's family. They simply may not have thought that they had committed any wrong, at least one that requires retaliation.

This entire event would most certainly be more understandable if we were given a little more detail on Dinah's role in the story. Unfortunately, we do not have that luxury.

3) Following the act with Dinah, the text states that Shechem spoke kindly to her, his soul was attracted to her, and he loved the young girl.

- Some scholars believe that this love was a mere sexual lust, instead of a heartfelt genuine love.
- Some believe that this "spoiled young son of a ruler" was just "taking what he wanted when he wanted, and by force if necessary." That this was not love, but the product of a selfish prince.

- But others take the text for what it says, and conclude that Shechem really did love this young girl.

It is worth noting, I believe, that the text states that his "soul was attracted to her." I don't know how much the soul is involved with sexual lust. However, I do believe that it takes part in genuine love. We learn later from the text that Shechem had kept Dinah. Shechem then asks his father to get Dinah as his wife.

5-7) The word had spread quickly. Jacob heard, but he wanted to keep his peace until his sons came in from the field. The sons of Jacob came running in from the fields, having heard the news themselves, and were less than happy about it.

8-12) Both Shechem and Hamor, his father, went out to meet with Jacob, and arrived to Jacob and his angry sons. Hamor, as leader of his tribe, proposes a combining of the two families. Following Hamor's suggestions would have gained Jacobs family full citizenship in Shechem. Such unity would be completely unacceptable to God. God was interested in separation from the pagan people.

- Some say that these men are attempting to "buy Dinah's virginity with money and a proposal of 'marriage.'"
- Some Scholars believe that Hamor has his own motivation. That he is motivated by the increase of possessions that would accommodate such an agreement for Hamor and his tribe. They point to verse 23 as evidence. In this case circumcision would be a small price to pay for such a grand reward.
- But still others believe there was, in fact, some honor and/or good will in the proposal.
- Shechem makes it clear that he is willing to pay any amount for Dinah.

13-17) Plotting on the basis of their practice of circumcision as a requirement for family membership, Jacob's sons deceitfully offer to form union with the Canaanites on this condition.

- It is possible that the sons of Jacob never dreamed of the Shechemites submitting to the conditions they laid down. After all, what an unreasonable thing to demand, that every male of the city be circumcised. Following their unwillingness, the sons of Jacob would take their sister back by force.
- It is also possible that the sons of Jacob did intend to commit the following acts. That they foresaw the acceptance of their demand of circumcision. That they had calculated the day of greatest pain and soreness to the defenders. That the whole design of their attack and victory was thought out in advance.
- Regardless of the intentions, Jacob's sons used a sacred ceremony, given by God, for a severely sinful purpose. Of course, mere carnal circumcision cannot make any nation worthy to share with them in their rare heritage.

19) *He was more honorable than all the household of his father* – This verse is interesting in light of what the context reveals. If he is a rapist, how is he honorable? At the same time, if his true affections are for Dinah and he has a loving soul towards her, it could fit. Also, could this simply mean that he was more highly esteemed by the folks at home? The ASV states, "He was honored above all the house of his father." Unfortunately, the actual definition of the word translated here as "honorable" won't help. Some of its definitions are as follows: to be heavy, be weighty, be grievous, be hard, be rich, be honorable, be glorious, be burdensome, be honored.

20-24) Although Hamor and Shechem had assented to the condition, they still had to convince the rest of the male population. Their arguments before their people went along this line:

1. Jacob's family was peaceable;
2. the land is big enough for both them and us;
3. we can trade and intermarry with them;
4. before this is possible we must consent to be circumcised;
5. this will be a small price to pay for we shall soon possess their substance and their flocks and herds.

25-29) On the third day, when the men of Shechem were incapacitated, Simeon and Levi entered the city and slew all the males. Shechem's crime, regardless of the circumstances, hardly warranted the brutal and extensive retaliation that it received. The shameful deeds of gross wickedness include:

1. They desecrated the sacred right of circumcision, making it the means of their brutal cruelty and murder of a whole city.
2. They shamelessly backed out of an agreement they themselves had proposed, doing so even after the Shechemites had kept their end of the bargain.
3. Their robbery of all the property and wealth of the city itself, as well as of all that was in the field was a horrible example of greediness.
4. They took captive all the children.
5. They "took" all the wives of the slain, a violation as sinister and damnable, if not more so, as the encounter with Dinah, thus multiplying endlessly the very sin they claimed they were avenging, and plundered their houses.
6. Never was there a darker day to cast its shadow over the people of God.

30-31) As a result of these actions, Jacob rebukes his sons for causing his name to "stink" among the other Canaanites in the land, fearing that some might seek revenge.

Shechem was Jacob's first stopping place in Canaan, on his return. There he bought a parcel of land, and erected an altar to God as if planning to make it his home, temporarily at least. But the bloody act of Simeon and Levi made him unpleasant to his neighbors.

Some think the excessive anger of the sons of Jacob should have been anticipated by Shechem. Throughout the east at that time, there was a generally held opinion that "A brother is more dishonored by the seduction of a sister than by the infidelity of his wife, because one may divorce a wife; but a sister or daughter always retains the relationship."

It is interesting to note here that the name of God ends chapter 33 and begins chapter 35, but it is completely absent from this sordid chapter in the life of God's people. Yet God's redemptive plan moved on. Scripture continues to record accurate and unbiased wrongs even of those in the covenant line.

Genesis – Chapter 35

Jacob's Return to Bethel

Intro) This chapter contains some interesting items in the life of Jacob. It marks the turning point in Jacob's life: his faith matures and he is able to take up the full mantle of his patriarchal calling. Some scholars, including Coffman, assert that the material is not in chronological sequence, but there does not seem to be anything in the chapter which demands that conclusion. The events recorded are:

1. The return to Bethel (Genesis 35:1-7)
2. The death and burial of Deborah (Genesis 35:8)
3. God's appearance again to Jacob, reaffirming the patriarchal promise (Genesis 35:9-15)
4. The death of Rachel in childbirth at the birth of Benjamin (Genesis 35:16-20)
5. The incest of Reuben with Bilhah (Genesis 35:22)
6. A list of the twelve sons of Jacob (Genesis 35:22b-26)
7. Jacob's final visit with Isaac and Isaac's death and burial (Genesis 35:27-29).

Jacob knows that the slaughter of Shechem's men has made them enemies in the region. At God's direction Jacob moves southward to Bethel, where Jacob had made a covenant with God on his way to exile in Haran.

Read Genesis 35:1-15.

1) God speaks to Jacob here and tells him to arise, go to Bethel, and dwell there.

- Bethel was a place where, 20 years before, in his flight from Canaan, Jacob had seen the heavenly ladder, and God had made him heir to the Abrahamic promises. Now God reassures him that those promises shall be fulfilled.
- After the violence at Shechem, Jacob and his family were certainly in need of spiritual renewal.
- As God had strengthened Jacob when he fled from Esau, so also as he flees from a likely vengeful wrath of the Canaanites, God upholds him.

2-4) As a preparation for this journey, Jacob demanded and received obedience from his family that they: (1) put away their idols; (2) purified themselves; and (3) changed their clothes.

- Among the idols mentioned here are most likely the stolen god's of Laban.
- The earrings which they gave to Jacob, were most likely used as idolatrous tokens or amulets (items used to bring good luck).
- The purifying process likely included ceremonial washing, abstinence from normal sexual activity, and contemplation.
- The changing of garments could have symbolized the putting away of old mistakes and being clothed with a desire for renewal.
- Now that the people have been consecrated by the three acts mentioned, Jacob's people can now approach Bethel to fulfill Jacob's vow and worship the Lord.

5) Instilled with the "terror of God," the Canaanites did not attack Jacob for revenge, as he had feared. Many times did God have to step in to protect and preserve his Chosen People. He meant what he had promised Jacob in Genesis 28:15. God, whom Jacob's family had somewhat forgotten and neglected, still protected them.

6-7) In keeping with his vow, upon his arriving in Bethel, Jacob dedicates the altar to God in gratitude for the divine care Jacob has experienced.

8) There are three deaths in this chapter of Genesis. The first mentioned is Deborah. This was Rebekah's former nurse. Because of her position, she must have been the subject of a great deal of respect and love to be mentioned here.

9-15) Just as God had appeared to Jacob at Bethel when he left Canaan, so also when Jacob arrived back at Bethel, God appeared to bless him. God again confirms to Jacob the covenant He established with Abraham. Here, Jacob's name change is reaffirmed also. The reminder is certainly appropriate following the spiritual low-point on the part of Jacob in Shechem.

Death of Rachel

Read Genesis 35:16-22a.

16-20) The second death mentioned in the chapter is Rachel, Jacob's beloved wife. Rachel gave birth to a son. Due to difficulties from the birth, Rachel died. However, before her death she named him Benoni, meaning "son of my sorrow." Jacob, possibly refusing to let the boy bear a name that was a constant reminder of grief, named him Benjamin meaning "Son of the Right Hand" or "Son of Days" (Son of my Old Age"). Following the death of Rachel, Jacob casts his deepest affections upon her sons, Joseph and Benjamin. Rachel was buried on the way to Bethlehem.

18) Notice in this verse the departure of the soul at the time of death.

21-22) This tells of yet another sorry episode in the life of one of Jacob's sons. Reuben lay with Bilhah, his father's concubine, Rachel's handmaiden. The Bible simply states the fact without elaboration. We are not even told what Jacob's reaction to it was, although we may be sure he strongly disapproved of it. This information gives us the necessary background for the statement of Genesis 49:3-4: "Reuben, you are my firstborn, my might, and the beginning of my strength, the excellency of dignity and the excellency of power. Unstable as water, you shall not excel, because you went up to your father's bed; then you defiled it— he went up to my couch." His character is mentioned again 1 Chronicles 5:1.

Jacob's Twelve Sons

Read Genesis 35:22b-26.

23-26) The six sons of Leah are named: Reuben, Simeon, Levi, Judah, Issachar, and Zebulun. The two sons of Rachel are given next: Joseph and Benjamin. Then follow the two sons of Bilhah, Rachel's maid: Dan and Naphtali. Finally, the two sons of Zilpah, Leah's maid, are named: Gad and Asher.

Death of Isaac

Read Genesis 35:27-29.

27-29) The third death mentioned in this chapter is Isaac, Jacob and Esau's father. We remember that once already Isaac felt death was near. Here we get the account of his passing from this life. Once estranged, but now reconciled, Jacob and Esau join to pay final tribute to their father, and bury him. Isaac lived 180 years, breathed his last, and was buried in the family tomb, in the cave of Machpelah.

* Rebekah's death and burial are not mentioned in the Scriptures. It is significant that while the mistress of the house is omitted from the Lord's obituary column, the lowly servant of the mistress has a rather prominent place. This shows that the Lord does not recognize the social distinctions which are so popular and meaningful to men. She was buried under an oak tree near Bethel. The place of Deborah's burial was called "Allonbachuth" which means "The Oak of Weeping," thus implying that her departure was accompanied with much weeping and mourning, and thus that she was a highly esteemed member of Jacob's household.

Genesis – Chapter 36

The Family of Esau

Intro) After recording the death of Isaac, and prior to shifting the attention to Joseph, the text briefly considers the genealogy of Esau, the less-favored son of Isaac. Due to being of only secondary importance in the covenant record, Esau's history is thus quickly disposed of before the story of Jacob's family continues. This is similar to the treatment of Ishmael back in chapter 25.

This is a concise account of Esau's descendants, who also belonged to the "many nations" promised to Abraham and Sarah. This brief account is given prior to the more full-blown account of Jacob's descendants.

The divisions of the chapter are as follows:
Vs. 1-8 – Esau's wives and children.
Vs. 9-14 – Esau's sons and grandsons.
Vs. 15-19 – Tribe-princes who descended from Esau.
Vs. 20-30 – Pre-Edomite peoples, descendants of Seir the Horite.
Vs. 31-39 – The Kings of the land of Edom.
Vs. 40-43 – Seats of the tribe-princes of Esau.

Read Genesis 36:1-14.

1) Esau is Edom

7) In this verse the text states, *"The land where they were strangers could not support them (Jacob and Esau) because of their livestock."*

- This was the same situation that existed between Abraham and Lot, resulting in their separation.
- Both examples show the divisive power that can be caused by great wealth, this being one of the ways in which wealth is considered by many to be wicked.

8) Because of the great wealth between the brothers, Esau moves and dwells in Mt. Seir.

The Chiefs of Edom

Read Genesis 36:15-19.

The Sons of Seir

Read Genesis 36:20-30.

20-30) The list given in verses 20-30 of the pre-Edomite inhabitants of Seir is of the greatest significance.

1. It reveals the manner of Edom's eventual amalgamation with the people through intermarriages with them, and finally coming to dominate the whole area.
2. What Esau did here through intermarriage with the Pagans of Seir, Jacob likewise could have done at Shechem; but the result would have been just as disastrous as it was for the posterity of Esau.
3. Sure, Esau took over the country, but the pagan culture of Seir took over the Edomites. Thus, the wisdom of God's providential interference, as some refer to it, with Jacob's continued residence in Shechem is demonstrated in this chapter.

The King of Edom

Read Genesis 36:31-39.

34) Jobab in vs. 34 is thought by some to have been "Job" of the book of Job.

1. "Eliphaz" and "Teman" are named in the book of Job.
2. This chapter may even supply the setting for the book of Job.
3. However, we are not certain of any of these claims, so we will leave them alone.

The Chiefs of Esau

Read Genesis 36:40-43.

Note: The Amalekites were a branch of Esau's descendants. They were the wandering tribe centered mainly around Kadesh in the north part of the Sinai peninsula. They were the first to attack Israel after the Exodus from Egypt, and they oppressed the Israelites during the period of the judges.

Note: The descendants of Esau later became bitter enemies of Israel, as is reflected in some of the prophets, especially Obadiah.

Genesis – Chapter 37

Joseph Dreams of Greatness

Intro) Following the brief account of Esau's family, the Genesis record focuses with greater detail upon Jacob and his descendants, for it is through the descendants of Jacob that the promised blessings are to come. Taking the leading role in the continuing saga is Jacob's son, Joseph. Jacob's special fondness for Joseph, and perhaps Joseph's own attitude, lead to envy and hatred by Joseph's brothers.

Read Genesis 37:1-11.

1) Jacob dwelt in the land of Canaan.

2) *This is the history of Jacob* – Despite the prominence of Joseph in this account, and his being elevated in order to preserve the chosen nation, he did remain subordinate to Jacob within the covenant structure. Therefore this text is the account, not of Joseph, but of Jacob, as it clearly states.

1-4) Joseph was hated by his brothers. This was due to several reasons that we will cover in this text. In verses 1-2 we read that Joseph brought a bad report of his brothers to their father, Jacob. In verses 3-4 we see the devotion that he enjoys. *"Now Israel loved Joseph more than all his children, because he was the son of his old age." "Also he made him a tunic of many colors."*

How strange it is that Jacob, who himself had been brought up in a household of foolish parental preferences between their sons, and who thus had accurate knowledge of the foolishness of such parental preferences, should have, himself, foolishly indulged in the same wickedness.

The coat was a symbol of favoritism. It possibly indicated Jacob's intention to make Joseph heir to the birthright. Reuben, Jacob's first-born, was natural heir to the birthright; but he was disavowed because of his illicit relation with one of his father's concubines. Simeon and Levi, second and third in the line of succession, were passed over because of their crime at Shechem. Judah, 4th son, was next in line; and it may have been expected, in family circles, that the birthright would fall to him. But Joseph, though Jacob's 11th son, was Rachel's first-born. Rachel was Jacob's best loved wife; and Joseph was his favorite son. So the coat may have looked somewhat suspicious.

Also, due to custom, it was a symbol that its wearer would not have to work.

5-11) Joseph has two dreams that symbolically portray his brothers bowing down before him. The relation of such dreams by Joseph to his brothers poured additional fuel upon the smoldering embers of their jealousy and hatred. It seems that Joseph was either ignorant of the effect his words would have on his brothers, or was egotistically pleased by it.

The second dream, he told not only to his brothers, but his parents as well. Some believe that this doubling of the dream was designed to indicate its certainty. Jacob immediately sees the dream's symbolism; the sun, moon and stars representing the father, mother (likely Leah, since Rachel was dead) and brothers respectively.

11) Jacob, due to his past experience and knowledge that dreams were one means of revelation, kept the matter in mind.

Joseph Sold By His Brothers

Read Genesis 37:12-36.

12-17) Joseph's brothers move on to Shechem to feed Jacob's flock. Israel sends Joseph to check on them. Once Joseph arrived at Shechem and did not find his brothers, he was at a loss to proceed. Luckily, he received help from a local. Though the brothers did spend time in Shechem, they had moved on to Dothan, approx. 20 miles north of Shechem. Joseph finally catches up with them there.

18-24) The brothers, still angry over Joseph's dreams and favored status with their father, plan to kill Joseph. Reuben, as Jacob's first-born, may have felt responsible for Joseph. So Reuben convinces them to throw him into a pit, alive, instead. His plan was to come back and retrieve his brother. This pit would have held water during the rainy season, but dried up toward the end of summer. This pit would have been impossible to escape from without help.

25a) As Joseph is in this pit, the text says that they sat down to eat bread. What a glimpse of unfeeling hardness is afforded here. These evil men were insensitive to the cries of their brother, which were most likely heard by them. They simply sat down to eat, apparently with no pangs of conscience whatever.

25b-28) The brothers then decide that, instead of killing their brother Joseph, they should sell him. Joseph is sold to a band of Ishmaelite traders.

- The text refers to Ishmaelites and Midianites here. Which were they? Ishmaelites or Midianites? Well, they were both! They were Ishmaelites by race, being descended from Ishmael, and they were Midianites by residence. The Midianites are also referred to Ishmaelites later in Judges.

Joseph was sold for 20 pieces of silver. Once you divide that up between the remaining brothers, we notice how cheap they held the life of Joseph.

29-30) Reuben had been absent during the sale. He returns to the pit and is upset that Joseph is no longer in it. As the oldest brother, he should have taken charge of the situation; and being the eldest, he would be looked to by Jacob to give an accounting.

31-35) After Joseph has been sold, the brothers return to Jacob, and lead him to believe that his favorite son had been devoured by wild animals. Today, the blood could be analyzed; and the goat's blood could not have been mistaken for human blood. In Jacob's age, the scheme was perfectly successful. Jacob was completely deceived.

Jacob was also devastated. It seems by the text that Jacob feels he may die from the grief.

Of course we remember that Jacob himself was the deceiver of his father Isaac, in the matter of procuring the blessing; and now, the deceiver is deceived. Jacob tore his clothes, put on sackcloth, and mourned the loss of Joseph.

36) At the end of the text, we notice that Joseph is then sold again to Potiphar, an officer of Pharaoh.

Here, then, is the conclusion of the events of this chapter, leaving Reuben filled with remorse, Jacob in perpetual mourning, and Joseph, the future savior of the nation, a slave to one of Pharaoh's officers in Egypt. The fortunes of Israel appear very low at this point.

Genesis – Chapter 38

Judah and Tamar

Intro) As Joseph becomes a slave in an Egyptian household, a most fascinating story is unfolding back in Canaan involving Judah, one of Israel's sons by Leah. It concerns the ancient custom of estates – quite foreign to modern thinking – in which the brother of a deceased man who has no children marries the brother's wife so that the brother's lineage and property may continue through a proper line of succession. Disgrace comes when Onan, one of Judah's sons, goes through the sexual act with his brother's wife, Tamar, but purposely prevents any offspring from being born.

Many scholars generally separate this particular chapter from the rest of the narrative, stating that "it is a completely different unit," and that "it has no connection with the story of Joseph." It is absolutely true that this chapter has nothing to do with Joseph. Remember, this is the genealogy of Jacob, not Joseph. As it relates to the subject of the whole section, it is most definitely not an independent unit. It pertains very significantly to the story of Jacob in his capacity as the head of the chosen nation.

Read Genesis 38.

1-5) Judah, Israel's son through Leah, separated himself from his brothers and went to live among the Canaanites in Adullam, southwest of Jerusalem. Judah marries the daughter of Shua and goes in to her. This must have been done without any real consultation with his father, Israel, and without any regard for the Canaanite nature of her father. Judah then has three sons through this wife: Er, Onan, and Shelah.

6) Though Judah married without any apparent parental consent, he nevertheless chose a wife for Er, possibly seeing that he had made a mistake in his own marriage. Judah choses a woman named Tamar to be Er's wife. Tamar, though possibly a Canaanite herself, may have been worn over to an acceptance of God by Judah. This could have been what made her acceptable to Judah. Later on she will be blessed in such a way that could give more significance to this suggestion.

7-10) Due to his wickedness; "the Lord killed Er" before he conceived any children with Tamar. This led to the following sequence of events. A quick note needs to be made here: It is now Judah's responsibility to take care of Tamar, not her father's.

1. The custom of the time was very simple. If a man dies and has no children, his brother is to take for himself the widow, marry her, and have children through her so that the estate of the dead brother would not pass to a different branch of the family.
2. Judah told Onan, his second son, to go into Tamar, marry her, and conceive children for the sake of his brother.
3. But Onan willfully disobeyed his father, shamefully disregarded the rights of his dead older brother, and perpetrated a heartless fraud against Tamar, who was most likely desperate for a child. He did this by allowing his seed to fall to the ground instead of conceiving with Tamar. Why did he do this?

       a. Selfishness? He did not want to preserve his brother's family?
       b. Greed? The estate of his father would have divided into two parts instead of three.
4. Due to Onan's actions, the Lord kills him as well, and Onan does not father any children.

We are not told how either Er or Onan die, however, we know that the wrath of God lay behind it. In fact, we are told in the Old Testament and the New Testament that the Lord killed those who were wicked. This instrument of God's wrath was never used without due cause; and in all the instances of it, some very grave danger to the covenant people was averted. That was certainly the case of the instance given here.

11) Judah promises Tamar that Shelah, his youngest son, will someday take her as his wife. We can notice from the text that Judah was afraid for Shelah's life, and that he would die as his other sons did. So it does not seem, by the circumstances, that Judah had any intention of giving his youngest son to Tamar. So not only has she been defrauded, in a way, by both husbands, she is now being lied to by her father-in-law.

12-19) Following the death of Judah's wife, Judah goes to shear his sheep in Timnah. When Tamar is told that Judah is going out to shear sheep, she chooses to disguise herself as a prostitute and position herself by the roadside, as custom would suggest. This entices Judah to stop and ask her to sleep with him. Before she agrees, Judah commits to sending a young goat from the flock and gives the girl his signet, cord, and staff as his pledge that he will return.

- The signet and cord could have been a small cylinder seal of the type used to sign clay documents by rolling them over the clay.
- The owner wore it around his neck on a cord threaded through a hole drilled lengthwise through it.
- What was most important to Tamar was that they would make it possible for her to identify the father of her child with absolute certainty.

20-23) When Judah returned, the sent the goat by his friend the Adullamite, and he was to return the pledge to Judah. However, she had left, and the men of the place said there had not been a harlot in that place.

If we inquire as to why Judah did not go to redeem the pledge himself, it would appear that he was ashamed to do so. Sure Judah lived in that type of society, but he knew better, and his conduct here seems to prove it. If they had made any further inquiry about the prostitute, it would have included more publicity than Judah probably wanted. All of this shows that Judah was, in some way, ashamed and wished, as much as possible, for it to just go away. Judah would get his signet and cord and staff back, but in circumstances he never dreamed of.

24-26) Three months later Judah learns of Tamar's pregnancy and orders her to be burned. Like many others, Judah was quick to see the sins of others a lot easier than he could see sin in himself.

According to some scholars, at this time stoning was the punishment given under normal circumstances for actions such as Tamar's. They say that burning was reserved only for daughters of priests who were condemned for adultery. If that is the case, it would appear that

Judah here exceeded the usual penalty by commanding that Tamar be burned. In later times, burning was the legal penalty for prostitution. What we can conclude is that Judah felt duty-bound to pass along the sentence against her.

In a climax that only Tamar could anticipate, as she is being brought forth for execution, she reveals the signet and cord and staff. This is the irrefutable evidence that the father of her child is none other than Judah himself. Can you imagine the shock on the face of Judah? Can you imagine the knot in his belly? There was no way for Judah to deny what he had done. So he admitted his shame. The red-faced Judah acknowledges, "She is more in the right than I am."

Note: As sinful as the deeds of Tamar were here, it is worth remembering that she is not motivated by lust. She is motivated by a lawful desire for children. In the light of subsequent developments, it appears that God overlooked her mistakes.

Note: Judah's immorality while away from home was shameful, but his acknowledgement of his sin and his acceptance of the consequences represented in him a type of honor absolutely unknown to the tribal leaders of that era.

27-30) Tamar gave birth to twins, who, as we have seen once before, did not come out quite as planned. Perez, who was planned to follow his brother in birth, broke through first. Zerah, who was marked with the ribbon as the first-born, followed behind his brother.

Note: Such immoral conduct that was found in this short story shows why it was necessary for God to remove the whole people from that environment. If the Lord had left Israel in Canaan, they would have most certainly fallen for the temptation of marrying with the daughters of the land, resulting in a great and rapid moral deterioration, resembling what we saw prior to the great flood.

Note: Little could Judah have realized that he had just become the father of a great multitude through Tamar. The most important aspect of this seemingly insignificant story will come to light only after many centuries have passed. At that time it will become evident that a descendant of Judah (through Perez) will become God's messenger to all mankind.

Genesis – Chapter 39

Joseph a Slave in Egypt

Intro) As Judah has been dealing with his various personal problems, his younger brother Joseph has been making the best of one disastrous situation after another.

The training received here by Joseph will be very helpful.

- In Potiphar's house he is trained in the Egyptian way of life and learns good business administration.
- His humiliation in prison will help him when he is promoted in Pharaoh's house.
- When his character is perfected, then, and only then, will he be ready to help perfect his brothers' characters.

Read Genesis 39.

1-5) Joseph becomes a faithful and highly effective servant in the house of Potiphar, captain of Pharaoh's palace guard. The key to the entire chapter lies in the text, "The Lord was with Joseph." In verses 2, 3, 5, 21, and 23 the same fundamental truth is repeated. The reader here is expected to see the hand of the Lord in these marvelous events. Joseph is in the house of his master. He did not live as a slave but was given very nice quarters as a reward for his good work. Joseph is master of his master's entire estate.

God was also blessing Potiphar just as He had blessed Laban because of Jacob. The offspring of Abraham continued to be a blessing to the nations. And just as Laban had entrusted his flocks to Jacob's care, Joseph had full responsibility for the welfare of Potiphar's house.

6) In verse 6 there are two points of interest worth noting.

1. Joseph did not have charge of Potiphar's meals. – There is no certainty as to why. Some speculation has been made that it was due to the strict caste laws of Egypt. Others believe that Joseph, as a foreigner, could not see to the preparation of food. This is based on the supposition that a foreigner would not have been familiar with all the religious rituals the Egyptians connected with eating. And others believe that it was neither, but that Potiphar would not trouble himself with anything other than his own eating.
2. There appears to be an unusual physical beauty that belonged to Joseph. This appearance of Joseph was probably inherited from his mother, Rachel. Genesis speaks in glowing terms of her beauty, using some of the very words used here.

7-10) Here we are told of a great temptation that Joseph is forced to face. Potiphar's wife looks with desire at Joseph and attempts to seduce him. Joseph rejects the advances of Potiphar's wife repeatedly. He even ran from the house on one occasion, leaving his garment behind.

What a temptation this would have presented to Joseph. The circumstances that he could have used in favor of this sin were numerous.

1. It could have been the means of his escape from slavery.

2. He could have felt that the wrongs that he had suffered entitled him to any revenge that was handy.
3. The prospect of secrecy was evident as there was no one in the house.
4. He was far from home, living in a culture that did not have the moral standards that he believed in.
5. It may have occurred to him that his refusal would have made his status worse.
6. And, most difficult of all to overcome, it was a continual and persistent temptation that was renewed every day.

Walter Russell Bowie said it like this, "A decent man can be shocked by the bold suddenness of evil, and his conscious may recoil; but when the shock wears off, the suggestion seems not so strange. Then comes a new danger. Just as a steel bridge which can resist a heavy blow may be endangered by the successive shocks that come from the feet of marching men, a man's moral resistance may disintegrate beneath the impact of temptation that comes relentlessly on and on."

Joseph, disregarding the circumstances mentioned above, fled from temptation. But what were his reasons?

1. It would have been an act of disloyalty to his master.
2. His master had not wronged him.
3. It would have been a wickedness (or sin) against God.

11-18) Having her advances rejected, Potiphar's wife resorts to vengeance. She is spurned and therefore hates him. And Joseph, having left his garment behind, sets the stage for her to falsely accuse him of attempted rape.

It is interesting to note that this is the second time Joseph's garment was made to lie wickedly about him. The first occasion was his brother's dipping his coat into the goat's blood to deceive Joseph's father.

19-20) The tradition handed down through Josephus is that Potiphar believed his wife's accusations. Despite this, there appears to be a bit of doubt about it.

1. The Scripture does not say that Potiphar was angry with Joseph. Perhaps it was caused chiefly by the vexation created by the whole bothersome incident. Since he could not disprove his wife's statements—it would hardly have done to take a foreign slave's word against his wife's—all that remained was to do the conventional thing and to punish Joseph and incidentally to get rid of a most efficient business manager.
2. The sentence executed upon Joseph was not expected for a slave for attempted rape of his master's wife. The death penalty was usual in such cases.
3. There is also the fact that Potiphar placed Joseph in a prison that was evidently under his own jurisdiction, which he did without any kind of trial, assigning the penalty under his own authority.

From these considerations, it appears that Potiphar accepted the truth of his wife's charges against Joseph with something less than total belief. He may have been more irritated than anything.

21-23) Joseph, after some time of being bound in prison, gains favor with the jailor, who places him in charge of the entire prison. Even in prison, Joseph enjoyed a measure of success through the help and presence of God. God was with Joseph and showed kindness to him. But let's not overlook the character of Joseph, who gained a remarkable degree of trust due to his work and trustworthiness.

As we read this particular chapter, we can notice some exceptional qualities of Joseph:

1. He was of unblemished character.
2. He was unusually handsome.
3. He possessed an exceptional gift for leadership.
4. He had the ability to make the best of every situation.

Note: This chapter stands as a refutation of the lives of those described in the preceding chapter. Judah was contaminated by his surroundings while Joseph was not. Just because Joseph leads the righteous life he cannot expect, and does not always receive, the best of treatment.

Genesis – Chapter 40

The Prisoners' Dreams

Intro) Imprisoned unjustly, but not downcast, Joseph gets the opportunity to interpret the dreams of the royal butler and the royal baker, who had been jailed after falling out of the king's favor.

Read Genesis 40.

1-4) While Joseph is in prison, Pharaoh's chief butler and chief baker anger him and are thrown into prison. Joseph is assigned to take care of them. Let us take a quick look at these two men:

- The chief butler: The title literally means "one who gives to drink." Because of the meaning of the title, the office is also referred to as the "cup-bearer." This was a highly-respected position because of the holder's access to the presence of the king.
- The chief baker: This official was responsible for seeing that the king's bread was both safe and appetizing. This official also held a high position of trust.

We are not told from the text what these men did to anger Pharaoh. And as always, where there is a lack of information, there is much speculation, and much speculation has been made about the manner of these men angering Pharaoh. These have ranged all the way from the allegation that they had plotted to poison him to some more trivial offense. From some Jewish writing we are given the following:

> *"The chief baker was put into prison because a pebble had been found in the pastry he baked for Pharaoh, and he was guilty of a misdemeanor because he had neglected the sifting of the flour. A fly had happened to fall into the wine that the chief butler poured for Pharaoh, but that could not be construed as caused by any negligence on his part. Thus, the butler had not committed a punishable offense."*

3) These two officers of the court were placed in the charge of the captain of the guard. This captain of the guard may have been Potiphar (39:1). The prison was located at the same site as Potiphar's palace, since these two new prisoners were put in prison in the house of the captain of the guard. This was the same place Joseph was being held. The keeper of the prison was the man in charge of it; Potiphar appears to have been the over-all superintendent of the prison as well as captain of the guard.

5-8) These two officials, while in jail, have dreams that they cannot understand. There were so-called "dream interpreters" in Egypt, however, the butler and baker were in jail so they had no access to them. Joseph acknowledges that only God, who knows the future, can properly interpret dreams. Joseph presents himself as God's agent through whom God will make known the revelation contained in their dreams. This shows that Joseph believed that God would in fact reveal the meaning of the dreams to him.

9-15) Joseph, after being told of the butler's dream, reveals to the cup-bearer that he will be released and restored to his position in three days. After revealing this information, Joseph asks the butler for a simple favor. He asks the butler to remember him and mention him kindly to Pharaoh so that he may be released from jail. Joseph feels that he had been stolen out of his homeland, and that he was not guilty of any punishable crime. And is confident Pharaoh would see his innocence in a review of his case. Unfortunately, though the butler is restored as Joseph had foretold, he promptly forgets Joseph.

16-19) When the chief baker saw that the interpretation was good for the butler, he told his dream to Joseph with hopes of the same. The news isn't good. Joseph reveals to the baker that he will be executed in three days.

20-23) The dreams of the butler and the baker are accurately interpreted by Joseph. At a birthday celebration for the king the cup-bearer is returned to his duty and the baker is killed.

A great deal of uncertainty focuses upon the exact manner of the baker's execution. Some suppose that he was first beheaded, and then impaled so that the remains could be seen. Others take the position that he was simply hanged. Either method would answer perfectly to the tenor of Joseph's interpretation of the Baker's dream.

Note: By this account we are able to see that God has not left the aid of Joseph, just as He said he wouldn't. God's aid, in this manner, will continue into the next chapter, and have greater consequences for Joseph.

Note: Now comes another injury (to Joseph), less malicious but hardly less disillusioning than the others. Here is a man he had befriended and helped. The chief butler did not set out to do him any harm; he simply did nothing at all. He just went off casually, and forgot. But to Joseph in prison, that was as hurtful as if it had been a deliberate wrong.

Genesis – Chapter 41

Pharaoh's Dreams

Intro) At this point, Joseph is still in jail, having been forgotten by the butler who was restored to his position. Little did Joseph know, he would soon have his own position of authority.

Read Genesis 41:1-36.

1-7) In the first of this text we are told that Pharaoh has two dreams. In the first dream, Pharaoh sees seven thin cows devouring seven fat cows. In the second dream, Pharaoh sees seven thin heads of grain devouring seven healthy ones.

8-13) Pharaoh, although he did call in his professional interpreters, could not find the meaning to his perplexing and disturbing dreams. Enter the chief butler, who suddenly remembers that Joseph was able to interpret his dreams. It had been two years since Joseph asked the butler to simply remember him before Pharaoh.

14-16) Joseph is brought from prison to hear the king relate his two mysterious dreams. Joseph is shaved and changed before he is brought out. This was required by the rules for those appearing before Pharaoh, but there is no doubt the change was refreshing to Joseph. The Pharaoh attempts to attribute some professional skill to Joseph giving him the ability to interpret the dreams. However, as he did with the butler and baker, Joseph hastily corrects Pharaoh's misunderstanding by attributing his ability to the aid of God.

17-24) Pharaoh reveals the dreams to Joseph.

25-32) Joseph, after hearing the dreams, begins his guided interpretation. He tells that both dreams represent the same event. Joseph reveals that Pharaoh's dreams are foretelling the events of the next 14 years. The first seven years will witness abundant crops, while the next seven will see only famine which will, in a sense, consume the first seven. A few points are worth noting:

1. It was unusual for Egypt to witness long famines.
2. This was due to the regularity of the annual overflow of the Nile.
3. This was most likely one reason why Pharaoh had such concern about the dreams. The vision of the river in the dream and the importance of it to their well-being would have certainly caused some concern.

33-36) Joseph suggests to Pharaoh that someone (a discerning and wise man) be appointed to store up food supplies during the years of abundance to prepare for the years of famine.

Note: Archaeology has discovered huge storage bins in Egypt which could be the very ones of this account.

Joseph's Rise to Power

Read Genesis 41:37-57.

37-44) Pharaoh liked the idea Joseph proposed and asked his servants if such a man, within whom is the spirit of God, could be found. Pharaoh then appoints Joseph, because of the aided ability and wisdom that he possessed, to oversee the storage of grain. This placed him in charge of the entire government in Egypt. This position was symbolized by Pharaoh's handing over the signet ring, dressing Joseph in fine linens, and placing the gold chain around Joseph's neck. Only in the throne, i.e. final, absolute authority, would Pharaoh be greater than Joseph.

In just 13 years, Joseph went from being hated by his brothers, thrown into a pit, sold to Potiphar, falsely accused of attempted rape, placed into prison, and now raised to this position of authority in Egypt.

45) Joseph is given Asenath as a wife. Asenath was the daughter of a pagan priest, she herself being named after one of the pagan goddesses of Egypt.

46-49) The first part of the dream comes true. Joseph stores massive amounts of grain in the nearby cities. There was so much grain that it was immeasurable.

50-52) Joseph has two sons, Manasseh, the firstborn and Ephraim. These men were later leaders in Israel's idolatry. There seems to be little doubt that the later idolatrous tendencies of Joseph's sons had originated with Asenath.

53-57) The second part of the interpretation comes true, a severe famine comes to the land. Because of the storing of food, when the famine comes, people from surrounding lands also come to Egypt to buy grain from Joseph.

This chapter sets the stage for the removal of Israel to Egypt, an event that begins to unfold in the very next chapter.

Genesis – Chapter 42

Joseph's Brothers Go To Egypt

Intro) The remarkable narrative of the events recorded in this and related chapters is extremely vivid, true to life, and charged with emotion.

Picking right up where chapter 41 left off, the famine is in full swing and Jacob, somehow, finds out about the food stored in Egypt.

Read Genesis 42:1-24.

1-5) Jacob tells his ten oldest sons, "I have heard there is grain in Egypt; go down to that place and buy for us there, that we may live and not die." Jacob did not send Benjamin with the brothers to Egypt. Rachel, Jacob's favorite wife, had died. Jacob also thought Joseph was dead. Jacob did not want to lose Benjamin, the remaining son of his beloved Rachel. There might even be some evidence here that Jacob in the intervening years had come to question some of the things his sons had told him. In any event, he refused to entrust Benjamin to them on this trip to Egypt.

6) When the brothers arrived before Joseph, they bowed down before him. This was the fulfillment of his previous dreams that had causing their hatred toward him.

7-8) Approximately twenty-one years had passed since he had last seen his brothers. Joseph recognized them. They were adults when they sold Joseph. Their appearance had likely not changed much. But why did Joseph's brothers not recognize him?

1. At the time of his enslavement, Joseph was 17. He was now an adult.
2. He was in an unexpected position of authority.
3. He was wearing Egyptian clothes and speaking to his brothers through an interpreter.
4. He was also shaven in the Egyptian manner.

9-14) We must conclude that, due to the number coming for food, that Joseph did not personally handle all of the details of so many sales. But, any group of strangers who might have been suspected of being spies would inevitably have been referred to Joseph, and this appears to have been exactly what occurred here. It seems the case of his brothers had been brought before Joseph personally by subordinates in the bureaucracy, and that they had originated the charge of spying. If so, this would account for two things: (1) Joseph's handling the case in person, and (2) the firm, even harsh manner in which he dealt with it.

It's worth noting here that anything on Joseph's part that could have been interpreted by lesser officials as disloyalty to Pharaoh would have been pounced upon and used by them against Joseph, for it may not be supposed for a moment that everyone in Egypt appreciated having "this foreigner" rule over them. Thus, Joseph discharged his duty under the circumstances to the fullest, openly backing up the false charges in a manner that left him above and beyond all possible criticism.

Joseph accuses his brothers of being spies. Their first response to this charge is that they are one man's sons. The argument here is that no father would risk sending ten sons on a single spy mission. The argument would have been a valid one. They also respond that they are honest men. I wonder how Joseph felt when he heard this from his deceptive brothers.

The accusation by Joseph referred to the "nakedness of the land." This had no reference to a lack of food supplies. There was plenty of food. This was referring to things that are meant to be hidden from potential enemies. The implication is that they had come to discover the state of Egypt's military preparedness to repel an attack. Testing their vulnerability, if you will. This is why the charge would have been taken so seriously.

15-20) Joseph, once his brothers have pleaded their case on the charge of spying, demands to see Benjamin, the youngest brother spoken of in the appeal. In their mind this was to prove their case before the governor and save themselves from a deadly penalty. Suspects in this day were considered guilty until proven innocent; therefore, the burden of proof was on the brothers. Originally, one brother would return and the rest would remain in custody.

To this point, Joseph had disposed of the case fully in keeping with what anyone in Egypt would have considered to be absolutely proper. After a period of three days, during which period practically everyone in Egypt would have forgotten all about the incident, Joseph would again review the case and reduce the number from ten to one of those who would be left in prison. Perhaps Joseph remembered the members of his father's house and thought of their dire need of food, and therefore he sent them all home except Simeon, their sacks laden with grain, and their money returned, as related at once by the sacred author.

21-24) The brothers began to feel that their actions are catching up with them. They begin to feel that God is punishing them because of their treatment of Joseph. Upon hearing his brothers, Joseph leaves the room so that he does not reveal his true identity as he weeps. Not only does Joseph hear his brothers discuss their own consequences and actions, he may also be hearing for the first time, that Reuben interceded on his behalf. This may be why Joseph had Simeon taken and imprisoned instead of Jacob's firstborn Reuben.

23) Joseph used an interpreter. Why? It may have been to help disguise himself from them. Refer to Isaac, Jacob, and Esau in 27:21-23.

The Brothers Return to Canaan

Read Genesis 42:25-38.

25-28) The nine remaining brothers arrive in Canaan with their food. As they unpack, they are astounded to discover in their bags the money they had used to buy the food. This gives them fear that they could now be charged with theft as well.

28) *What is this that God has done to us?* – Why blame God? They knew they were responsible for what happened to Joseph. It seems it is natural for men and women to look elsewhere to place the blame for their own faults and calamities. It happened with God's people then and it happens within the church today.

29-38) They tell Jacob all about their trip, including how "the man" (Joseph) has requested that Benjamin accompany them on their return journey.

Jacob replies to them in absolute and final terms: "You have bereaved me of my children." "Joseph is no more." "Simeon is no more." "You want to take Benjamin away." This is total accusation – in that the loss of all three would be the fault of these men. He doesn't even know how close to the truth he was!

Reuben's rash promise about slaying his two sons as a surety made no impression at all upon Jacob. Jacob is not willing to part with Benjamin for fear of losing him.

Genesis – Chapter 43

Joseph's Brothers Return With Benjamin

Intro) This chapter is a continuation of the remarkably dramatic history that began to unfold in the last chapter. When the food runs out for the second time, Jacob is forced to relent on his refusal to allow Benjamin to go to Egypt.

Read Genesis 43.

1-2) Jacob's determination not to send Benjamin back into Egypt with the brothers will have to give way under the dire necessity for the procurement of food. The famine grew worse, and although he had no information about how long it might last, there was simply no other way to provide for the children of Israel.

3-7) We remember from the previous lesson that the brothers were to return with Benjamin to give proof that they were brothers and not spies. We also remember that Joseph said, "You shall not see my face unless your brother is with you." So if there was no Benjamin, there would be no food purchased from Joseph. Judah reminds Jacob of that very demand.

8-10) After Judah guarantees Benjamin's safety, a reluctant Jacob finally agrees to let Benjamin go. Judah offered himself as security for Benjamin's safety. This was certainly an even more generous gesture than that of Reuben who offered his own sons.

The biblical account does not tell us fully why Jacob consented to what Judah suggested. However, we get an adequate idea from Josephus who tells us that Judah pointed out to him that Benjamin could just as well die without food, and appealed to Jacob on the basis of faith in God.

11-13) Jacob puts together a gift for the Egyptian official consisting of balm, honey, spices, myrrh, pistachio nuts, and almonds. He also sends a double offering and commands the brothers to pay for the grain first received as well as for new purchases.

14) Finally, Jacob decides to rely upon God, instead of his own devices and precautions. Until now, Jacob saw only the problems and difficulties; he did not discern the providential hand of God in these heartaches and hardships. And he sends them away with his blessing. Jacob would accept whatever consequences came of the situation with faith and resignation.

15-17) When Joseph saw the men and Benjamin, he sent them to his home, where food would be prepared for them. There is no doubt this was a shocking surprise.

18) The fear that the brothers express here is certainly understandable. Joseph is the chief deputy of the all-powerful Pharaoh, he is supreme in Egypt, and no doubt lives in a place befitting his rank and authority. The fact that these travelers from the land of Canaan were invited into such a place was no doubt an occasion for the most dreadful apprehension and fear, especially considering their previous encounter.

19-22) Supposing that the money found in their sacks after their first journey might be an occasion for their seizure, they sought to put that matter to rest in advance by returning the money to the steward.

23-25) The steward's answers must have confounded and confused them even more. The manager of Joseph's household reassures the frightened brothers that his master means them no harm and that their God had been the provider. From this, it appears Joseph's steward was aware of his master's faith in God, and that possibly, to some extent, at least, he himself shared it.

Simeon is then released and joins them in the house. The men are not treated as criminals but as guests. They were given water, their feet were washed, and their donkeys were fed. Meanwhile, They have their gifts ready for Joseph.

26-31) When Joseph comes home, the men greet him with the present that had been prepared. Twice on this occasion the brothers prostrated themselves before Joseph, thus fulfilling the dreams that Joseph dreamed so long ago. These were the dreams that had precipitated the hatred of his brothers. After inquiring about the brothers' father, Joseph 'introduces' himself to Benjamin. The text, in verse 29, specifies that Benjamin was, "his mother's son." The special relationship between these two is made clear once again. At this point, Joseph's emotions almost overpower him, but he left the room to weep. After regaining his composure, he returned to order the dinner.

32) So the occasion is set, and preparation is made for the upcoming meal. There were at least three tables set for the participants of this feast. First, Joseph ate by himself, due to his rank and authority. There was another table for the Egyptians present, for whom it would be an abomination to dine with the Hebrews. The taboo was likely based on ritual and religious reasons. Then there was a third table set for the Hebrews.

33) *And they sat before him, the firstborn according to his birthright and the youngest according to his youth.* – Nearly every scholar, that I have noticed, is of the understanding that Joseph had these men placed in this order. This leads to the great astonishment mentioned at the end of verse 33. However, when you take the custom, the circumstances, and the text for what they are, it is just as possible, maybe even more so, that these men were simply told which table to sit at, and were not placed individually in their respective order.

The text gives detail to the fact that these tables were set separately and the reasons for this are understood. Then it says, "They sat before him, the firstborn according to his birthright and the youngest according to his youth." So where does the astonishment come from? Well let's see.

- A. These men came home from their first trip to Egypt with food and the money that they had taken to buy it. This caused a fear that they would be charged with theft.
- B. They arrive again before the Egyptian governor and he has them sent to his home. This, in their minds, arouses greater fear that they will be punished severely due to their theft of the monies.
- C. Don't forget that these men have been thinking this whole time that their past dealings with Joseph are beginning to catch up with them, and that God is likely to punish them because of them.

D. When the men arrive, not only are they not in trouble, they are treated as honored guests. Their brother Simeon is returned, they are given water to drink, their feet are washed, and their donkeys are even fed.
E. Not only are they treated as honored guests, these Hebrews are treated this way in the home of the Egyptian Governor, by his servants, and in the company of other Egyptians. They are then placed before him to eat food that has been prepared for him. This food is then taken off of his table and placed on theirs.

So I believe, due to the series of events, astonishment is a likely emotion for these men. You may decide for yourself which angle you would like to take.

34) It seems this may be a trial for the brothers, to see if they were still jealous of Rachel's children.

Genesis – Chapter 44

Joseph's Cup

Intro) After feasting and learning more about his father, Joseph dismissed them with renewed stores of grain, but also orders that his own silver cup be secretly placed in Benjamin's sack. Shortly after leaving the city, the brothers are stopped and searched. To the brother's horror, the cup is found in Benjamin's sack, and he is arrested.

Read Genesis 44:1-17.

1-5) Joseph sends the brothers back on their way home but does two things. He puts their money back into their sacks again and also puts his silver cup in Benjamin's sack. Many questions arise with Bible scholars as to the reason behind this. McGarvey has a comment that I believe is relevant. He suggested that Joseph desired to have his only full brother at his side, to enjoy the full benefits of his own exalted status in Egypt. This view explains why he demanded that the brothers bring Benjamin with them when they returned for more grain.

One of the points of interest here is the matter of that silver cup and Joseph's use of it for "divination." Whether Joseph is conceived of as really practicing divination, or only wishing his brothers to think so, does not appear here. I would not consider it out of reason that he actually did so. After all, his mother Rachel did steal the false gods of her father. Some say Joseph would have been more apt to use this as a mere ruse to convince the brothers that they could not trick him. But we just simply don't know for sure.

Many have mentioned the various ways of divination by means of a cup. Sometimes, "Such a divination cup was filled with water, then oil was poured on the water; and the future was predicted on the basis of the forms that appeared on the surface. Mesopotamian sources indicate that ... water was poured into oil, or fragments of silver and gold were dropped into water or oil, and a priest or diviner read the message in the way the globules arranged themselves."

The eleven brothers were sent on their way as soon as it was light. They would naturally be in the best of spirits as they began their journey homeward: they had had the honor of eating at the house of the great man of Egypt; they had been reunited with Simeon; they had not met with any difficulty in the matter of the returned money; they had been able to obtain plenty of food to take home; and nothing evil had befallen their brother Benjamin. Their fortunes appeared to be on the rise. Unbeknownst to them, Joseph was instructing his steward to pursue after them, and demand why they had stolen his silver cup.

6-9) So the steward overtakes the brothers and accuses them. The brothers claim innocence and their arguments are those of innocence. First, they argued that they had already returned the previous monies found in their sack. Then they said "With whomever of your servants it is found, let him die." We notice that this is the same response given years earlier by Jacob to Laban when Rachel stole the pagan gods. And finally, if one is found guilty, the rest shall become slaves.

10) The steward changes the agreement; only the guilty is to be bound! It seems as if he is aware of Joseph's plan.

11-13) The brothers were certainly tested by Joseph when the cup was found to be in Benjamin's sack. Here, since the steward had changed the agreement with the brothers, they had the opportunity to leave Benjamin, much like they did Joseph years earlier, but they resolutely refused to do so. They rent their clothes, but keep their vow and return to the city.

14-15) Once again, before Joseph, they threw themselves down, fulfilling further the dreams that he had before. Joseph then confronts the brothers.

16-17) Judah speaks up for the group, confirming their original pledge. However, Joseph, calling attention to his faith in God, stated that he would not punish any innocent people: only the man who had the cup would become his servant; the rest could return to their father. Again, they could have abandoned their brother but would not!

16) *God has found out the iniquity of your servants* – Judah by this could not have meant that they were in any manner guilty as charged with reference to the cup. The thing that had haunted the guilty brothers for twenty years was their sinful, unmerciful hatred of their brother Joseph.

Judah Intercedes for Benjamin

Read Genesis 44:18-34.

18-34) This is the pinnacle of the Joseph story. Here, after recounting the whole story, Judah stands forth begging Joseph to release Benjamin, offering himself as a sacrifice to spare the life of his brother. This happens at a time when he might have supposed that Benjamin could have been guilty. After all, the cup was found in his sack. This likely helped to make amends for his role in selling Joseph.

What a transformation had occurred in the life of Judah! Standing before his very eyes, Joseph saw that same hard-eyed brother who had once mercilessly sold him as a slave into Egypt standing there pleading with all of his heart to be made a slave forever in the place of Benjamin! Such a scene was never known before, and Joseph's heart was simply broken by it.

Henry M. Morris' comment on this passage is:

> *"In this willingness to give his own life in place of his brother's, for the sake of his father, Judah became a beautiful type of Christ, more fully and realistically than even Joseph himself, who is often taken by Bible expositors as a type of Christ. Hereby perceive we the love of God, because he laid down his life for us: and we ought to lay down our lives for the brethren."*

Genesis – Chapter 45

Joseph Revealed to His Brothers

Intro) After Judah pleads for the sparing of his brother Benjamin, Joseph simply cannot hold his emotions back any longer.

Read Genesis 45:1-28.

1-2) Unable to hold back any longer, a tearful Joseph clears the room and reveals his true identity to his astonished brothers. Joseph here only wanted the decent privacy that all men desire upon occasions of deep emotion.

3) The text reveals that the brothers were dismayed at Joseph's presence. The meaning of this is "to tremble inwardly" or "to be alarmed". They had already been exposed to the rough treatment and words of which the great ruler was capable; now understanding him to be their brother whom they had treated even more harshly, and knowing the great power he now possessed, they could only anticipate vengeance.

4-8) Joseph tells his brothers not to worry about what happened in the past. He tells them that though they were the ones that sold him to the Egyptians; it was God who sent him into Egypt. He was sent by God to preserve their posterity [remnant] with a deliverance from the famine.

- a. Without Joseph's influence in Egypt, most of Jacob's family would have likely died in the famine.
- b. Remember, this is only 2 years into the famine and they had gone to buy food twice already. The news that the famine was to last five more years had not been available to the brothers until Joseph mentioned it here.
- c. Also, it was because of Joseph's suggestion to store the food during the years of plenty that afforded Egypt the stored grain that they survived on and sold.

Joseph recognizes that, through his brothers' jealous and cruel acts, God had a purpose to work.

9-15) Joseph then tells his brothers to go home and tell their father to pack up and move to Egypt. They are told to move to Goshen. Goshen was a fertile region located on the eastern section of the Nile delta. This was considered the "best of the land of Egypt".

16-20) There are a few points worth noting when Pharaoh finds out about the visiting brothers.

1. The fact that Pharaoh did not require any elaboration as to who "the brethren" were, shows that Joseph had most likely already informed him of who they were.
2. Pharaoh not only ratified and confirmed Joseph's words to them, but he put the invitation in the form of a command, and added an offer of wagons to aid the transport of the women and children.
3. This shows that Pharaoh was not only aware of Joseph's situation with his brothers, he was also, probably because of the great service Joseph had shown to Pharaoh and his people, happy to aid in the effort.

21-24) Joseph provides the men with provisions for the journey. He also gave Benjamin 300 pieces of silver. This was a very substantial gift. The price of a slave was thirty shekels of silver (Exodus 21:32). This gift was the equivalent of a gift of ten slaves.

25-28) The brothers return to Jacob and tell him that Joseph is alive and that he is governor in Egypt. Jacob is hesitant to take the brothers at their word to begin with. In fact, he states frankly that he does not believe them. But then, as he was told the words that Joseph spoke, Jacob looked back and saw the wealth being brought to him. Once he saw them approach, he believed and was ready to see his son.

It is notable here that Jacob did not seem to be impressed with the fact of Joseph's being a ruler in Egypt, but only with the fact that he was alive.

* Right here, the die is cast. Jacob and all the children of Israel would go down into Egypt, where the long sojourn God had foretold to Abraham would begin. One scholar stated:

> *"What a wonder is this record of how it happened! God overruled the hatreds, jealousies, and envious wickedness of men to place one of Jacob's sons on the throne of the land of Egypt, who, in time, brought the whole posterity of Israel to live there. The Egyptians detested foreigners, especially shepherds; and, thus there would be no easy possibility of Jacob's posterity forming marriages with pagans, as had already begun to happen in the case of Judah. Not only that, in Egypt, they would have the protective arm of a powerful central government which would secure them....Under those divinely appointed conditions, they would indeed grow into a mighty nation!"*

Genesis – Chapter 46

Jacob's Journey to Egypt

Intro) This is a pivotal chapter in the history of the Chosen People. It relates the transfer of the entire nation into Egypt, fulfilling, in part, the prophecy of God to Abraham (Genesis 15:13-14).

The move of Israel into Egypt was no small matter. First, there was a great deal of planning and work involved to transfer the entire household, together with the tents and other goods, and all the flocks and herds belonging to this wealthy family. Then there was the emotional issue of departing from the land promised to them through Abraham to go into an alien country. However, on the positive side, there was the prospect of being with the beloved son Joseph, and being near to the food necessary to sustain life.

Read Genesis 46:1-27.

1-4) Israel began his journey and came to Beersheba, where he worshiped God. Beersheba was on the southern limits of the promised land. It was perfectly logical that worship be offered before fully taking leave of Canaan. Isaac had lived at this place and had erected an altar there; it may be that Jacob sacrificed on this very altar.

God then speaks to Jacob. God says:

1. I am your God, the God of your father.
2. Do not fear to go into Egypt.
3. I will make of you a great nation.
4. I will go with you.
5. Joseph will be with you until your death.
6. You will not be buried there.

In other words: God will be with Israel until he dies.

Jacob may have been having second thoughts about entering Egypt prior to God's reassurance.

- We remember that Egypt was a place of shame for Abraham. This is where he deceived Pharaoh saying that Sarah was his sister.
- We remember that Isaac was forbidden by God to enter Egypt during the famine that struck him.
- Jacob may have been recalling the ominous revelation made to Abraham back in chapter 15 when he was asleep.
- But God sets Jacob's fears at rest by informing him that entrance into Egypt is harmonious with His purposes.

As far as the record goes, this is the last time God appears to Jacob, having appeared to him 8 times in all.

1. 28:13
2. 31:3
3. 31:11

4. 32:1
5. 32:30
6. 35:1
7. 35:9
8. 46:2

It is worth noting that the appearance of God to Jacob did not come for the personal benefit of the patriarch, but it was upon occasions pertinent to the welfare of the covenant nation. For example, God did not appear to Jacob and comfort him with regard to the fact that Joseph was indeed alive during the years that he thought Joseph was dead.

In verse 4, God informs Jacob that it will be Joseph who puts his hands upon Jacob's eyes. This is a prophecy that Joseph shall perform the last rites at his father's death. The closing of the eyes in death was a rite anciently performed by the hands of a loved one. In colonial America, after loving hands had closed the eyes, coins (usually nickels) were placed upon the eyes till rigor mortis ensued. From this came the proverb for a petty thief: "He would steal a nickel off a dead man's eyes!"

5-7) Jacob obeys God and goes down to Egypt. Pharaoh had said that they could leave all their goods back in Canaan, but verse six shows that Jacob had brought all their possessions with them, as well they should. God had provided them with all these things, so they could not simply abandon them. Also, their specific tools and goods might not be readily available in Egypt. Further, since promises are often made which are soon forgotten, it was wise to bring what they could instead of trusting the Egyptians to provide for their needs. Jacob brought all his possessions and family.

8-26) The listings of the family:
Leah: 6 sons + Dinah
             2 sons by Zilpah
Rachel: 2 sons
             2 sons by Bilhah
             12 sons in all.

27) Jacob and his entire family move to Egypt. But we need to make a brief note about the list given in the text. The grand total given is 70. This list does not include any of the daughters, except Dinah and Serah, despite the mention of his (Jacob's) daughters. Note also in these verses that nothing whatever is said of the wives of Jacob's sons and grandsons, nor is there any reference to their servants or employees. From this, it is evident that the company which went down into Egypt was far larger than the list of barely seventy persons, the whole list being contrived by the narrator as a "round number." The great intention, therefore, of this list is to show that there were seventy founders of the nation of Israel who went into Egypt.

Jacob Settles In Goshen

Read Genesis 46:28-34.

28-30) As the great company neared Egypt, Jacob sent Judah on ahead to learn the exact location in Goshen they were to settle. What a remarkable picture: the procession of Joseph in the Second Chariot of Egypt with full honors of the nation, going up to greet his father and welcome him into the land of Goshen! Father and son, Jacob and Joseph, reunite and embrace. Joseph weeps with gladness. And Jacob, maybe thinking that death is near anyway, is more ready now, having been reunited with his long-lost son. He would live 17 more years (Genesis 47:9, 28).

31-34) Pharaoh had invited them to come without regard to possessions left behind (Genesis 45:20). At the end of the chapter, Joseph, while speaking with his brothers and his father's household, informed the brothers to stress their occupation as shepherds. Joseph had foreseen that Goshen was the correct place for his father's people. It was primarily pasture land with scant, if any population. It also provided the isolation the Hebrews needed if conflict with the populations of Egypt was to be avoided.

Joseph knew well that the Egyptians, because of their low regard for nomadic shepherds, would not desire to have the Israelites right in their midst. So he urges his family to confirm and stress their occupations as shepherds so that the king will authorize their settlement in the fertile, outlying region of Goshen. This is where Joseph desired to settle them, and the interview went exactly as planned.

Genesis – Chapter 47

Jacob Settles In Goshen Cont'd

Intro) This chapter is so obviously related to the migration to Egypt that we shall consider it merely as an extension of the theme in the last chapter.

Read Genesis 47:1-12.

1-6) The formal permission of Pharaoh was required for the family to be able to settle in the land, and this interview afforded the occasion for that. It also gave Pharaoh the occasion to formally welcome them into the land.

Joseph presents five of his brethren to Pharaoh. Joseph had correctly discerned the question Pharaoh would ask the men. They obey Joseph and state they are shepherds and ask for Goshen to settle in. Pharaoh not only says he will allow the settlement, but he gives them control over his cattle too.

Note: Despite his having oversight of all Egypt, Joseph did not undertake this settlement of his folks in Goshen without the formal consent of the ruling monarch.

7-10) As Jacob and Pharaoh come together for the first time, they have a brief exchange, followed by a blessing of God given to Pharaoh.

9) *The days of the years of my pilgrimage are one hundred and thirty years* – Here is a glimpse of the way Jacob viewed his life. Neither he nor his father ever owned any of the land of promise except the burial place at Machpelah and a few acres around Shechem.

Few and evil have been the days of the years of my life – This is not a reference to Jacob's wickedness but to the severe and trying experiences which life had brought to him. Not all of the terrible experiences were the result of his own doing, but some were: the preference that his father had for Esau; his purchase of the birthright; the ensuing hatred of Esau; the shameful treatment he received from his father-in-law, Laban; the long years of servitude in the outdoors; the unhappiness of his wives due to internal conditions in his family; the hatred of his sons toward Jacob's favorite, Joseph; their sale of Joseph, represented to Jacob as Joseph's death; rape of Dinah; the shameless massacre of the Shechemites by two of his sons; Reuben's incest with one of Jacob's wives; the bitter famine; the imprisonment of Simeon; Jacob's horror upon learning Benjamin would have to go to Egypt; the following anxiety about him ... all these things left their mark upon the heart of Jacob, hence, his reference to them here.

11-12) Pharaoh gives them Goshen and Joseph carefully attends to the needs of his father, Jacob. Joseph personally sees to it that his family has all the food they need. Joseph also grants a possession of the best of the land as Pharaoh had commanded.

Joseph Deals with the Famine

Read Genesis 47:13-26.

13-14) This is the first of three stages during the latter years of the famine. All the money was gathered from the residents of the land. It had simply run out.

15-17) This was stage two. The first solution given by Joseph was for the people to sell their livestock for food. This was not the plan of a heartless man who was willing to take every advantage of the emergency. Rather, he was doing them a favor: if they could not feed themselves they could not feed the animals. But the government was able to take proper care of the animals. This allowed for food, but only temporarily. It is generally accepted by scholars that these residents received their livestock back later.

18-26) This was stage three. All the Egyptians (except for the priests) are then forced to sell their land and themselves to Pharaoh for food. Joseph then redistributes the land and establishes a law requiring one-fifth of all crops to be given to Pharaoh. Joseph's wisdom and position during this time of famine were enhanced in the eyes of the king and the people.

Note: The priests of Egypt were exempt and Pharaoh provided their sustenance for them.

Joseph's Vow to Jacob

Read Genesis 47:27-31.

27-31) As this chapter comes to a close, we have Jacob's request to be buried back in Canaan. The act of putting the hand under the thigh, as we have mentioned before, accompanied the taking of a solid vow. Jacob demands that Joseph swear to him. This matter is so important to Jacob that Joseph's promise is not enough; Jacob demands the promise be sealed with an oath. Joseph swore an oath to Jacob, and Jacob bowed himself on the head of his bed. This exchange shows the utmost confidence that Jacob had in the word of God which had assured him that his posterity would not remain in Egypt. "By faith Jacob, when he was dying, blessed each of the sons of Joseph, and worshiped, leaning on the top of his staff" (Hebrews 11:21).

Genesis – Chapter 48

Jacob Blesses Joseph's Sons

Intro) Now that Israel is nearing death, he is anxious to pronounce blessings upon his sons and grandsons, especially now that he has ensured that his burial would be in the tomb where Abraham and Isaac were buried.

Read Genesis 48.

1-4) A message is given to Joseph reporting his father's illness. We are not told how much time had passed since the events of the preceding chapter, merely that it occurred "after these things." It is likely that this was only a short time before the death of Jacob, in view of the fact that he is pictured as seriously ill. Joseph took his two sons with him when he went to visit his father. If this is shortly before Jacob's death, then Manasseh and Ephraim were about twenty years of age.

Jacob gives Joseph the message revealed to him by God. This message was given to Jacob both in chapter 28 & 35 that he will be fruitful and multiply, that from him will come a multitude of people, and this land will be given to his descendants as an everlasting possession. Of course, everlasting being conditional of their obedience (cf. Deuteronomy 28:15-25).

5-7) Jacob legally adopts Ephraim and Manasseh, Joseph's two sons and makes them equal to his own. This gives Ephraim and Manasseh equal inheritance with Jacob's other sons. This also gives Joseph a double portion of the inheritance. To stress this equality, Jacob compares their position to that of his oldest biological sons, Reuben and Simeon.

There were many reasons why Jacob had decided to do this. The incest of Reuben and his irresponsibility had clearly disqualified him to receive the double portion, and Simeon too, in the massacre of the Shechemites had showed a disposition that was incompatible with any thought of transferring the birthright to him. Jacob therefore decided to give Joseph the double portion, one of the principal benefits pertaining to the birthright, an honor that Jacob surely felt that Joseph was qualified to receive.

Not only was Joseph the firstborn of Rachel, the only wife that Jacob ever decided to marry, but, additionally, he was the savior of the whole nation in being the instrument through whom God had preserved the covenant people through the famine. Had Rachel not died while giving birth to Benjamin, she may have borne Jacob more children. By adopting Ephraim and Manasseh, Jacob has made an increase to the "tribes of Rachel".

8-20) After asking that the boys be brought to him, Jacob attributes their presence to the goodness of God. Israel embraced and kissed these two boys, saying to Joseph that he had not even thought he would be able to see Joseph again, but God had been so merciful that he not only saw him, but his sons also. Notice the gratitude expressed to God.

Joseph presents his sons to Jacob in a manner where Jacob would have reached out with his right hand naturally and placed it on Manasseh. However, Jacob crossed his hands to place the right hand on Ephraim. The placing of the right hand was a sign of favoritism. So Manasseh, being the first born, was who Joseph expected to get this sign. Joseph tries to correct Jacob in the reversed blessing. But Jacob states that he is well aware of what he is doing. He states that he placed his right hand on Ephraim because he would receive greater blessings than Manasseh.

From several scholars we are informed of several characteristics of the type of blessing Jacob was here bestowing upon the sons of Joseph:

1. It was a very formal, solemn, and serious affair.
2. If the one conveying it was empowered by God to do so, it carried with it the power to achieve what was promised.
3. When the blessing was uttered, it was irrevocable.
4. The patriarch always asked the identity of the one who would receive the blessing.
5. Those to be blessed were invited to come forward.
6. The recipient(s) was(were) embraced and kissed.
7. The right hand of the patriarch rested on the head of the one to receive the greater blessing.

This sheds light on the reason for Jacob's asking the identity of Joseph's sons in v. 8; it was a part of the formal procedure and did not mean that Jacob had never seen them before.

Note: It was not the gift of nature that determined the passing of God's blessing to one person or to another, but the sovereign purpose of Almighty God. Again and again a similar thing had happened in the lives of the patriarchs.

1. Isaac the younger had been chosen over Ishmael.
2. Jacob the younger had been chosen over Esau.
3. Joseph the younger had been chosen over Reuben.
4. And now Ephraim the younger had been chosen over Manasseh.

Note: It is worth noting that this is the first example in the Bible of the laying on of hands in the act of blessing or the conveyance of a gift. Afterwards, the act was extensively employed, but this is the first example we have.

21) The action of Jacob in blessing Ephraim over Manasseh became a proverb in later times. He promised Joseph that God would indeed bring his family back into Canaan. He did not mention any time factor, but stated it would be after his own death.

22) *Portion ... which I took from the hand of the Amorite with my sword and my bow* – Jacob is not presented in the Bible as a warrior, however he plainly states what he had done in this instance. There are generally two lines of thinking regarding this statement. The first is that this is a reference to an event which is not otherwise recorded in the Scriptures. The others think it was prospective in nature and was fulfilled later when Israel conquered the land.

Genesis – Chapter 49

Jacob's Last Words to His Sons

Intro) Now we have the final prophecy and blessing of the twelve tribes by Jacob their father. This has been referred to by some as one of the most magnificent passages in the entire Bible.

Read Genesis 49:1-28.

1-2) Jacob calls his sons together to hear what he has to say about their future. This must have been a very important date and event in the memory of the family for many years.

Jacob had known his sons all their lives; he knew their strengths and weaknesses. In his closing moments, he was able to bring this knowledge to bear with the divine guidance of God to formulate a final concise message to each of these sons who were the foundation of the great nation of Israel. This final word from the grand old patriarch was needed by Jacob's descendants as they approached the dismal days of bondage under the cruel taskmasters of Egypt. By the use of it men of Israel could look forward to the blessed time when the tribes would be safely established in the Promised Land, every tribe in its own inheritance.

3-4) Reuben – The natural love of Jacob for his firstborn appears in this prophecy to Reuben. God had promised Jacob that he would be made into a great nation; and Reuben was the beginning of the fulfillment; but, alas, the firstborn, in this instance, was not destined to live up to all the high hopes his father had in him. Because of his immorality, going into his father's bed, he actually receives a demotion.

It should be noted that Jacob's pronouncement here was fulfilled exactly in all the subsequent life of Reuben. He never furnished a leader of any kind to the nation. His was the first tribe to ask for a place to settle, and that before they ever entered Canaan (Numbers 32). They erected an unauthorized place of worship (Joshua 22:10-34). In the days of Deborah and Barak, his tribe violated their pledge and refused to answer the call to arms (Judges 5:15-16).

5-7) Simeon and Levi – Due to their anger and consequential violence, these two will be scattered throughout Israel. Since the cooperation of these brothers had produced some very shameful results, God would divide them. The background of this prophecy is the conduct of these two brothers in the events hinging upon the defilement of their sister Dinah. Jacob's plea was that his soul and honor might not take part with their evil ways.

In the case of Levi the situation is different. The Levites were, indeed, dispersed throughout the whole land in the cities mentioned in Josh. 21:1-40. But in their dispersion these ministers of the sanctuary served as teachers of Israel and so really became a wholesome leaven, whose influence was felt for good by all. Of course, the turn for the better in the case of the Levites came with Exod. 32:26ff.

8-12) Judah – Judah is the first of his brothers to receive commendation and a beneficiary blessing. The right of the first-born, taken from Reuben because of his sin and withheld from

Simeon and Levi due to their violence, is in part granted to Judah, the fourth son. Judah is predicted victory over his foes. Judah is granted authority over his brothers. This tribe became dominant, and from this tribe came such great ones as David and Solomon, and it was from Judah that Jesus sprang (Hebrews 7:14). The mention that "your father's children shall bow down before you" indicates that not merely the children of Judah's natural brothers (the other sons of Leah) would be subject to him, but that all of Israel would likewise be. His land and its inhabitants will prosper greatly. The scepter (royal line) will not depart from him until the coming of the One to whom it belongs.

This is a prophecy that the right of rulership shall pertain to the tribe of Judah; but this did not come to pass at once. Moses was from Levi, Joshua from Ephraim, Gideon from Manasseh, Samson from Dan, Samuel from Ephraim, and Saul from Benjamin. However, in the long sweep through history the prophecy was completely fulfilled only in Judah and the house of David, one of Judah's descendants whose reign prefigured the everlasting kingdom of the Messiah.

13) Zebulun – His land will be strategically located so that his descendants might prosper from commercial activity. In fact, the city of Sidon would enjoy commercial prominence.

14-15) Issachar – Jacob's sixth son and his tribe are pictured as physically strong but lacking in courage and ambition. Their complacency would make them prefer to accept oppression and task-work rather than fight to maintain freedom and independence.

16-17) Dan – Jacob's first son by Rachel's handmaid will be a deadly adversary. He will be like a snake beside the road. The thought here is that Dan, although few in number and not strong militarily, would nevertheless be able to overcome by cunning strategy.

18) This is an interruption in the process of blessing his children. He has stated the various natural strengths of some of his sons: Judah the lion, Issachar the strong donkey, Dan the cunning serpent. There were also many hardships, disasters, and conflicts awaiting his posterity. In this timely statement, the patriarch appeals to the Lord for the help he alone could provide. Jacob understands that though man may have natural strengths, success ultimately depends on God's mighty hand.

19) Gad – Jacob predicts that Gad's descendants will be bothered by marauding bands but will ably defend themselves.

20) Asher – He and his descendants will receive a very fruitful land which would produce rich delicacies. In 1 Kings 5:11, it is revealed that Asher lived in the lowlands along the Mediterranean between Carmel and Tyre, a fruitful and fertile region; and Solomon supplied the household of King Hiram from the wheat and oil products of this region.

21) Naphtali – The meaning of this prophecy is simply not clear. Few details are given concerning this tribe other than their part in defeating the army of Jabin (Judges 4-5; cf. Deborah's song). The reference may be to a characteristic of swiftness on the part of the men of this tribe. The figure used to describe them is also used in 2 Samuel 22:34 to illustrate fleetness of foot: "He makes my feet like the feet of deer, and sets me on my high places."

22-26) Joseph – Joseph's tribes, like Joseph himself, will meet strong opposition, yet with trust in God's power his tribes can overcome, as Joseph himself overcame. The source of this victory will be the true God, successively pictured as the Mighty One in whom Jacob trusted, the divine Shepherd who leads men, and the strong and sure Rock on which Israel relies. Many types of blessings, including blessings of climate, fertility, and human fruitfulness, are thus bestowed upon Joseph, Jacob's favorite and most illustrious son.

27) Benjamin – Jacob intended no criticism of his youngest son. Benjamin would be successful in the ferocious manner in which they would deal with the enemy. Among those of this tribe who lived up to this standard were Ehud (Judges 3:15) and Saul (1 Samuel 11). The whole tribe had this characteristic, although not always in the right cause (cf. Judges 20). Saul of Tarsus was a member of this tribe (Phil. 3:5). He was fearless and strong in his dealings with enemies of the gospel.

28) So Jacob blessed each of the boys, according to his blessing. That is, guided by the unerring Spirit of prophecy, Jacob now foretold to each of his sons all the important events which should take place during their successive generations, and the predominant characteristic of each tribe, and, at the same time, made some comparatively obscure references to the advent of the Messiah, and the redemption of the world by him.

Jacob's Death

Read Genesis 49:29-33.

29-33) In his final charge, he commanded them to bury his body in Machpelah where his father and grandfather had been entombed. He had already placed Joseph under oath to ensure he was buried there, but now he includes all his sons in this demand. After confirming his request to be buried with his ancestors in the cave of Machpelah, Jacob draws up his feet and breathes his last. Jacob does not forget that the land of his ancestors is his homeland appointed by God. This is also the place where Abraham and his wife Sarah, Isaac and his wife Rebekah, and Leah, the wife of Jacob were buried. Though nothing is said in the text as to when Leah died and was buried, only here, in the Bible, do we learn that Jacob had buried Leah in Machpelah.

Jacob's age is not given at this point, but he had already spoken of it when he was before Pharaoh in Genesis 47:8-9, at which time he was one hundred and thirty years of age. Genesis 47:28 shows that he lived in Egypt for seventeen more years, dying at the age of one hundred and forty-seven. So the earthly life of this great patriarch was over.

Genesis – Chapter 50

Burial of Jacob

Intro) As this Period of history comes to a close, we witness the burial of Jacob, the reassurance of Joseph, Joseph's final charge, and his death at the good ole age of 110.

The story of Jacob's burial is told in a rather detailed fashion, more so than is any other burial except Sarah's in the book of Genesis (chapter 23), because it gives a fine example of faith on the part of the patriarchs. Jacob desired burial in the land of promise, thereby testifying to his faith in the promise.

The entire material of the chapter is an excellent preparation for the book of Exodus.

Read Genesis 50:1-14.

1-3) Following the death of Jacob, Joseph had his servants and physicians embalm his father. There were a couple of reasons for Jacobs being embalmed. First, a long period of mourning was scheduled. There was also the necessity to transport the body over a great distance to the land of Canaan.

What about the embalming process? Dummelow, a scholar, had the following:

> *The brain and intestines were removed, and the stomach was cleansed and filled with spices. The body was then steeped in a mixture of salt and soda (called natron), for forty or more days, to preserve from decay. Next, it was bound up in strips of linen smeared with a sort of gum; and finally it was placed in a wooden case, shaped like the human body, and deposited in a sepulchral chamber.*

4-5) As the days of weeping for his father came to a close, Joseph went and spoke to Pharaoh, through messengers, regarding his commitment to return to Canaan and bury Jacob. But why did he use messengers? There are a few possibilities, but none that we can be dogmatic about.

1. Some say that since the burial of the dead was closely connected with their religious rites, He approached Pharaoh through the priests who were principals in the house of Pharaoh.
2. Some say that since Joseph was a mourner, he was unclean, and because of this appearance he could not see Pharaoh personally.
3. Some suggest that another Pharaoh, not so friendly to Joseph, had ascended the throne.
4. Some state that it was simply due to diplomatic considerations, which is not unreasonable since the request involved Joseph's leaving Egypt.

6) Pharaoh ultimately agreed to allow Joseph to return and fulfill his commitment to Jacob.

7-9) The sheer size of the pageant was most impressive. Those who went were: The houses of Joseph; the brothers; the house of Jacob; all of Pharaoh's servants; the elders of Pharaoh's house; all the elders of the land of Egypt; chariots and horsemen.

It is quite apparent in this that Pharaoh did not grudgingly consent for Joseph to leave and bury Jacob, but on the other hand supported the mission greatly. Josephus even tells us that all of this was done "at great expense."

10-11) Another period of mourning was had for Jacob, lasting for seven days. The mourning offered by such a large company so impressed the Canaanites in the vicinity that they gave a new name to the place: Abel Mizraim ("The Mourning of the Egyptians").

12-14) This chapter records the burial of Jacob by the side of Leah, instead of Rachel, his favorite wife. It is possible that Jacob finally accepted the rightful place of the long-despised Leah as actually his true wife. Clyde Francisco suggested this:

> *After the death of Rachel, Leah had Jacob alone for a number of years. Did she finally win his love, and did Jacob see that her love was far more meaningful than the fitful passion of the more beautiful Rachel? We cannot tell for certain; but this passage hints at Leah's ultimate victory over Rachel.*

In connection with this, it should be recalled that Judah (Leah's son) emerged as the spiritual leader of Israel, that the Messiah came through Leah, and that, at last, in the cave of Machpelah, her body rested alone by the side of Jacob.

Joseph Reassures His Brothers

Read Genesis 50: 15-21.

15-18) Here we see that the brothers of Joseph are afraid that revenge will be brought upon them now that Jacob has died. They allege that Jacob gave the commandment, to be sent through them, that we see in the text. A number of scholars see nothing unreasonable with such an allegation; but considering the text, it simply does not ring true. If Jacob had wanted to give Joseph a message about forgiving his brothers, it seems he would have given the message to Joseph himself. He certainly had the opportunity to. And too, these brothers were known for deceiving and lying already. Remember the coat dipped in goat's blood? John T. Willis has this to say:

> *All this looks suspicious, and it is difficult to avoid the conclusion that Joseph's brothers invented this story in a desperate effort to assure their own safety.*

19-21) The important outcome of this was that Joseph had forgiven his brothers, and probably long before the event related here. Joseph recognized also that it is not his prerogative to judge men and to punish them for their injustice to others.

19) *You meant evil against me; but God meant it for good* – There has never been a more vivid picture of the providence of God than in these words of Joseph to his brothers. He was not saying that God caused them to think evil against him, for they were responsible for their own thoughts. But God, in his wisdom and power used their evil purpose to achieve his will.

Death of Joseph

Read Genesis 50:22-26.

22-24) So the period of the Patriarchs, and similarly the book of Genesis, comes to a close with the death of its last chief character, who expresses prior to death a strong trust in God's plans for the people of Israel. Joseph is also embalmed so that he may be carried froth when God shall visit them and they return to the Promised Land.

25-26) The outstanding thing in this whole chapter is the conviction of all of Jacob's sons that God, in time, would remove them from Egypt and bring them into the Promised Land. This appears in verse 17, where the brethren of Joseph referred to themselves as "the servants of the God of your father." It appears again here, where Joseph refused to be buried in Egypt and took an oath of the children of Israel that they would take his remains with them when they went into Canaan. This last request would be honored by the Israelites. They would eventually carry out his remains in the Exodus and bury him at Shechem.

Close: In this marvelous narrative, the principal purpose was that of outlining the providential manner in which God brought about the separation of the Hebrews in order to bless "all the families of men," how He providentially overruled the sins, hatreds, failures, and disobedience of men in order to achieve His purpose, and how, for thousands of years, He guided the Chosen Nation to that hour when the angels of heaven would shout over the hills of Judea, "Glory to God in the Highest ... for there is born to you this day in the city of David a Savior which is Christ the Lord."

About Mitch

Mitch Robison is a Gospel minister, a missionary, a husband, a father, and a servant. A native of Georgia, he currently serves as the pulpit minister for the Pleasant Grove Rd. church of Christ in Inverness, FL.

Mitch began his studies at the Georgia School of Preaching in 2008. In 2009, he began to serve the Cedar Grove church of Christ in Fairburn, GA as their associate minister. He is grateful for the great Christians there who taught him so much about being a genuine man of God.

In 2015 Mitch began work as a full-time minister for the Enon church of Christ in Webb, AL. He served there for 2 ½ years, continuing to grow in knowledge of the Scripture. The time at Enon allowed him to begin emphasizing his mission mindedness. He organized several mission efforts locally and within the southeast region.

In 2018 Mitch began to serve the Christians of the Pleasant Grove Rd. church in Inverness, FL. This opportunity has allowed him to have continued growth in many aspects of his Christian walk, including his focus on authentic Christianity and missions, both in the community and the region.

In 2004 Mitch married his beautiful wife Katy. She has served by his side as an encourager, teacher, and example of an authentic Christian woman. In 2008, they were blessed with their daughter Sadie (Mitch had been hoping to have a little girl). In 2011, their son Eli was born. Mitch takes a lot of pride in Eli and strives daily to be a positive example of a Christian man to his son.

If you have a desire to contact Mitch, feel free to do so!

Phone – 678-953-1510
Email – mitchpgr@gmail.com
Mail – 5641 S. Burr Terrace,
Inverness, FL 34452